Beginner's Guide to

Goldwork

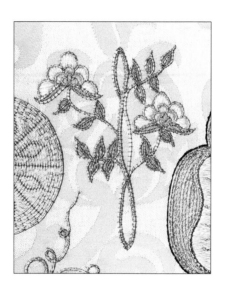

I dedicate this book to my family. To my husband Peter who has always encouraged me in my work all through our married life, and who has typed all the script for this book. To my daughter Anna who has been so kind and helpful in travelling with me, encouraging me, and sharing a lot of fun along the way! To my son Timothy who has always been behind me in whatever I have undertaken, and to my daughter-in-law Jacqueline who has kindly taken time to read portions of the script.

Beginner's Guide to

Goldwork

Ruth Chamberlin

SEARCH PRESS

First published in Great Britain 2006

Search Press Limited
Wellwood, North Farm Road,
Tunbridge Wells, Kent TN2 3DR

Reprinted 2007, 2008, 2009, 2011

Text and embroidered designs copyright © Ruth Chamberlin 2006

Photographs by Charlotte de la Bédoyère, Search Press Studios;
Roddy Paine Photographic Studios; and Henry Allen (pages 1, 32,
33, 51, 53 and 63).

Photographs and design copyright © Search Press Ltd. 2006

ISBN 978-0-85532-954-9

The Publishers and author can accept no responsibility for any
consequences arising from the information, advice or instructions
given in this publication.

Readers are permitted to reproduce any of the items in this book for
their personal use, or for the purposes of selling for charity, free of
charge and without the prior permission of the Publishers. Any use
of the items for commercial purposes is not permitted without the
prior permission of the Publishers.

Suppliers
If you have difficulty in obtaining any of the materials and
equipment mentioned in this book, then please visit the Search
Press website for details of suppliers: www.searchpress.com

Publisher's note
All the step-by-step photographs in this book feature the
author, Ruth Chamberlin, demonstrating her goldwork
techniques. No models have been used.

Reproduction by Altaimage London
Printed in China

Acknowledgements

*I would like to thank the Sisters of Bethany for their
kindness in photographing and allowing me to use Sir
Ninian Comper's lovely cope hood in this book; V&A
Images/Victoria and Albert Museum for allowing me to
reproduce the Syon Cope on pages 8 and 9; Henry Allen,
who photographs my work with such care and sensitivity;
Angela Taylor, who frames all my work with such
understanding and great skill; Benton and Johnson, who
supply all my gold threads, and, until she retired recently,
Kath Moore, who could not have been more helpful over
any request made; Wendy at Mace and Nairn, who is so
wonderfully efficient and reliable with any order given for
filofloss and other embroidery requirements; Pearsalls for
their wonderful range of coloured filoselle silks; Perkins
and Sons for their help and guidance over many years
and for the wonderful fabrics they produce; Watts and Co.
for supplying fabrics for so many years; Mulberry Silks
(Patricia Woods), who supplies spools of beautiful threads
in many thicknesses; Silk Route, who supply beautiful silk
fabric in varying thicknesses and textures; BWH Designs,
Whitby for supplying the slate frames that I use; Keith
Lovell, who is an authority on Comper and who has been a
tremendous help and encouragement to me; the Art Shop,
Oakham where I obtain all my art materials and where
Chris is so helpful; and Search Press for their kindness and
enthusiasm, especially Roz Dace and Katie Chester who
have been wonderful to
work with.*

Contents

Introduction 6

Materials 12

Equipment 18

Design 20

The sampler 22

Getting started 24

Stitches 34

Laid stitch 36 • Couching 38 • Trellis stitch 41

Padding 42 • Satin stitch 44

Decorative leaf design 46

Long and short stitch 48 • Brick stitch 50

Golden diamond design 54

Golden circle design 56

Diamond design using two colours 58
Kid 60

Three circles design 62

Decorative lozenge design 64

Teardrops design 66

Raised gold 68 • Basket stitch 70

Acorn project 74

Index 80

Introduction

I was delighted to be asked to write this book, as goldwork is the art form I love the most. After a general art school training at Croydon School of Art, I originally chose to study Dress. It was the 1950s, people were aglow with post-war optimism, and the need for more excitement in their dress was apparent. The delight I gained in designing and making clothes during this time was enormous, but having worked at Worths of London for eighteen months I soon began to realise that the world of dress was not for me. Although I loved the excitement of the fashion world, I yearned to draw and to work in a field that was less frivolous and more lasting. I was told about the School of Embroidery, Lloyd Square, London which provided training in Ecclesiastical Embroidery. Even though the leap from high fashion to the concentrated and minutely detailed work I would be doing at the embroidery school was enormous, I decided to go.

Having made the change it soon became clear that I had made the right decision. The work was tremendously challenging but completely absorbing, and I very soon realised that the standard of work was extremely high. Sir Ninian Comper was the church architect who used the school for the working of many of his embroidery designs, and I have included a section on his inspiring work on pages 10–11.

All the work at the embroidery school had to be of the highest possible standard – indeed, although I have been on many courses since, and have trained to teach, I have never seen a higher standard of work anywhere – and so I began the long process of learning all the techniques of silk embroidery and goldwork. When I began to teach I produced the sampler which is shown on the cover and on page 23 of this book. It includes the many techniques which I learnt while at the embroidery school, and has proved an invaluable teaching aid over the years. It is therefore a great pleasure for me to share my sampler with you by using it as the basis for this book. Once you have taken the time to master the techniques (and it is very important that you do so), I hope it will inspire you to combine all that you have learnt with your own ideas on design and colour to create a sampler of your own.

Christmas

This embroidery is shaped in the form of a bauble. The design within the bauble, in which the star of Bethlehem touches the Christmas rose, emphasises the real meaning of Christmas, and the outside of the bauble, which is highly decorated, reminds us of the joy and fun that can be had at this time.

The Opus Anglicanum

Opus Anglicanum is the name given to English embroidery during the thirteenth and fourteenth centuries. For me, it was the most inspiring period in the history of goldwork. Indeed, when Sir Ninian Comper mentioned that the work at the School of Embroidery, Lloyd Square, London, run by the Sisters of Bethany, 'should follow as closely as possible upon the lines of the Old English work in its best days', I feel he, too, could have been thinking of the expertise found in the work executed so many years before during the Opus Anglicanum period. The work was of a tremendously high standard, very sought after by the church officials at that time, and costly, because of the use of silver, silver gilt threads and precious stones and pearls. It is thought that the design for a lot of the work of this period was taken from the illuminated manuscripts and was drawn by the artists who worked on them.

The embroidery itself was often referred to as 'acupicture' (painting with a needle) and was carried out by highly trained and skilled professional embroiderers who were employed in workshops in London.

The picture opposite is of the Syon Cope, made between 1300 and 1320AD. The ground of this cope is a linen fabric and the whole of the background is covered in an underside couching. This technique involved laying silver gilt thread on the surface of the fabric and stitching over it with, in this case, a red and green silk thread. The thread was then pulled through the fabric, taking the loops to the underside, then the needle brought up at equal intervals to give an equal surface stitch. This method achieved a very malleable and serviceable texture, and when you look at this piece of work it is almost impossible to believe how such intricate work could be attained, particularly under what must have been very hard and difficult circumstances.

If you visit the Victoria and Albert Museum in London, you will see this and many other examples of the Opus Anglicanum period, carefully preserved and cared for by the conservators for us to see, to wonder at, and to enjoy.

Syon Cope

By kind permission of V&A Images/Victoria and Albert Museum.

Sir Ninian Comper

The work of Sir Ninian Comper has influenced me greatly, and I feel honoured to have been one of the last pupils at the School of Embroidery, London to have worked under this influence. Sir Ninian began to design for the embroidery school in 1886, and he did this until the end of his life in 1960. Designs for vestments, banners and altar frontals were drawn and executed by the school using textiles that were woven and dyed to his design and specification, and the school soon became known for its excellence.

Sir Ninian Comper travelled extensively, gathering ideas as he went from looking at paintings and architecture. He particularly loved Flemish paintings and you can certainly see in his drawings and fabric designs the influence that these paintings had upon his work. Colour was all important to him, and he would go to great lengths to obtain exactly the tone and depth of colour he needed. He was known for his own particular shade of mauvy pink, which was dyed to his specification and called 'murray'. This wonderful colour can be found in all his larger designs. Another characteristic feature of his work was that the figures of the Saints or the figure of Our Lady would always be standing on what was called a 'garden'. This would be of a charming shape, worked with brick stitch around the edge, with small but beautiful flowers (usually of different colours and shapes) worked in floss and surrounded with fine Jap gold thread. If the figure were seated (as in the cope hood illustrated opposite) he would add to this design a 'pavement'. This would usually be of a symmetric design worked in black and white floss, or in this example blue and murray floss outlined with Jap gold.

As you look at this exquisite cope hood, designed for the Sisters of Bethany in 1936, you can see that the design and workmanship of the embroidery is quite spectacular. As a young art school student, I just could not believe that any hands could have worked it, for the intricacy of the shapes and the beauty of the stitchery are immense. The cope hood was worked on a blue silk damask called St Nicholas and finished with a half-inch pure silk fringe which was dyed to match. This piece was, and still is, the most wonderful inspiration to me and I hope so much that it may be to others too.

The face of Our Lady and the body of the Christ Child were worked in long and short stitch using three threads of floss, each as fine as a single hair. These were very carefully twisted together when used. When a slightly warmer tone was needed, perhaps for the cheeks or lips, two threads of flesh colour and one of a slightly warmer tone were used together. For the eyes, the pupil was worked first and then surrounded with a tiny back stitch in a circular movement. The robe was worked in solid brick stitch, and you will see that the gold threads lay in the way dictated by the folds, with the deeper folds being achieved with closer stitchery. The cloak lining was worked in a chevron stitch using blue floss, with the Fleur de Lys embroidered in a fine Jap gold. The cushion was worked in a beautiful green floss in long and short stitch, which takes your eye to the tiny sash around Our Lady's waist. The ermine on the cloak was worked in long and short stitch with satin stitch markings in black. The halo (or nimbus) was worked in Jap gold thread over shaped padding.

Cope Hood
By kind permission of the Sisters of Bethany.

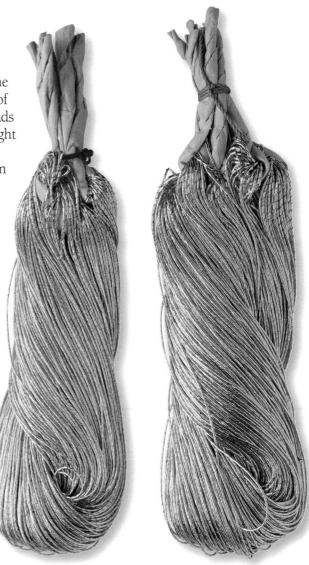

Materials

As with any new subject you wish to pursue seriously, you have first to consider the materials and equipment you need in order to proceed. There are those items you must have, of course, but gold threads and embroidery silks can be bought gradually as your work dictates.

Gold threads

In the early days of ecclesiastical embroidery, silver gilt threads were used frequently: they were easily available but costly. Nowadays there are many and varied gold threads available. Jap gold is the first to mention as it is the most precious and is glorious to use. It is made in Japan of pure gold leaf bound around a pure silk thread. The threads vary in thickness from very fine to thick, and they are bought in hanks (shown in the picture opposite). Jap gold has a wondrous quality and comes in various gold colours, from pinky gold to a more lustrous gold colour.

There is now an extremely good imitation gold thread on the market which is used extensively. It is called imitation Jap gold. Like Jap gold, it comes in various thicknesses and colours. It is lovely to use, is much less expensive than Jap gold and will never tarnish. Sold on reels, there is a huge variety of imitation gold threads and cords available, some of which are shown on the facing page. As you progress it is exciting to experiment and see how they can be incorporated into your embroidery to give many different effects and textures. This is where the joy of using these gorgeous threads comes in!

When starting a sampler, I always suggest that my students use two metallic threads known at T69 and T70 (one thick and one finer). These threads are easier to manipulate when you are a relative beginner: they do not slip too much and will make a sharp corner when required! This metallic thread can tarnish, but only after a long time. Once this thread has been mastered, you can progress to using imitation Jap gold.

As a general rule, the correct way to use gold thread is to use two threads together. It is therefore important to be able to use the appropriate thickness. If the design is very large and bold, the thickest gold thread, which is called K1, is used. If a small and delicate shape is to be either filled or surrounded, a finer thread, either K4 or K5, is required.

When using Jap gold or imitation Jap gold, it is always advisable to handle the gold thread as little as possible (hands can become hot however careful you are!). When using Jap gold, some people prefer to make a roll of felt and then to wind the thread on to it. Personally I prefer to shake the hank when using this gold to obtain two threads with which to work, making sure that enough has been undone to enable me to work comfortably. I then lay the hank at the side of my work. When using imitation Jap gold I use two reels, taking a thread from each and making sure that the reels are in a safe position on my frame.

I think silver threads should be mentioned here. Real silver thread will tarnish quickly but there are various aluminium threads on the market. These can look cold when used on their own, but mixing threads can be very exciting and can help the tonal effect enormously. When storing gold and silver threads, it is advisable to line the box with black acid-free tissue paper.

The other imitation gold threads to mention here are pearl purl, check purl, bright check purl, rough purl, smooth purl, gold coloured twist, rococo thread and gold plate. Some of these are shown below. They come in gold, silver and copper, and some pearl purl is made with a quantity of real gold in it.

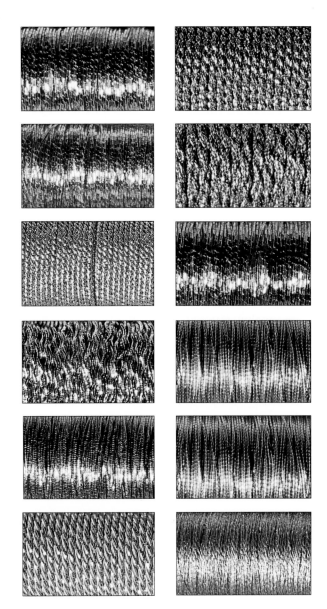

A selection of imitation Jap gold threads.

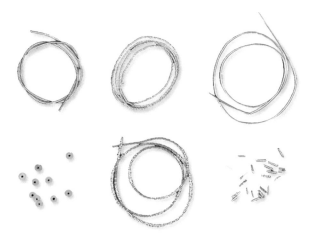

These threads can be cut to form beads of different lengths. Pearl purl can be pulled and, when sewn, used as a border. Plate can be sewn on the surface of the fabric, and usually a rough purl or perhaps a bright purl (cut like a bead) sewn at intervals over the top. This method is called Burden stitch.

Coloured threads

As an ecclesiastical embroiderer I have used many different threads in my work, and as I am basing this book on my sampler it is important to mention all the threads I have used for couching and for the different embroidery stitches.

I usually use a silk thread when couching gold threads down, but there are times when I have not found the colour needed in a silk thread and so have had to use a synthetic thread instead: colour is all important to the finished piece! Threads come in varying thicknesses and so it is important to find the right thickness for the work being undertaken.

To embroider the different stitches shown on my sampler I use both pure silk floss and twisted embroidery silks. Floss comes in skeins packaged on card. The finished thread is made up of six fine threads and one or two threads are used as required. Pure silk twisted thread is also packaged in skeins. In this case I find it helpful to undo the skein and cut it in half (this gives the right length of thread to use in your needle) and then to plait it together loosely, tying each end with a contrasting thread. (It is always advisable to keep the number of the thread used as a reference.) You are then able to pull the appropriate number of threads required for the work being undertaken: always pull your threads from the same end. The range of colours obtainable is magnificent.

Twisted embroidery silks.

Pure silk floss.

Silk threads used for couching.

Kid

Kid is made of real leather and comes in different colours: bronze, silver, and a variety of gold colours and textures. I prefer to use it sparingly. It comes in varying thicknesses – always choose the thinnest you can sensibly use.

Needles and pins

I use a No. 9 or 8 sharps needle for couching, depending upon the type of thread used, and a No. 10, 9 or 8 sharps needle for the floss work depending upon the level of fineness required. Embroidery needles have a larger eye and can be used if preferred. Nos. 14, 16, 18 and 20 chenille needles are used for passing gold threads through the surface of your work. Steel pins which are fine and strong can be used; also pins with coloured heads are useful as they can be seen easily. They also come in differing lengths and strengths. When sewing kid you will need a fine needle. I like using a sharps No. 10 for this task. (Use a No. 10 embroidery needle if you find a sharps No. 10 too fine to thread.) For lacing your embroidery frame, you will need a tapestry needle or a strong rug needle.

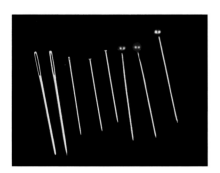

Shown here, from left to right, are a tapestry needle, a chenille needle, a fine sharps needle, two steel pins and three pins with coloured heads.

15

Fabrics

The fabrics that can be used for goldwork are extremely varied. I use a lot of pure silk damask for my ecclesiastical work. Some of these silk designs have been woven for many years and are still being woven today. The fabric designs are all named and are very beautiful to look at and to use. I always feel that it is important when placing a design on to a fabric of this sort that you use the background design to the best advantage: the silk can enhance the embroidery design enormously. You can see an example of this on the facing page.

A selection of pure silk damasks that I have used extensively for my ecclesiastical work.

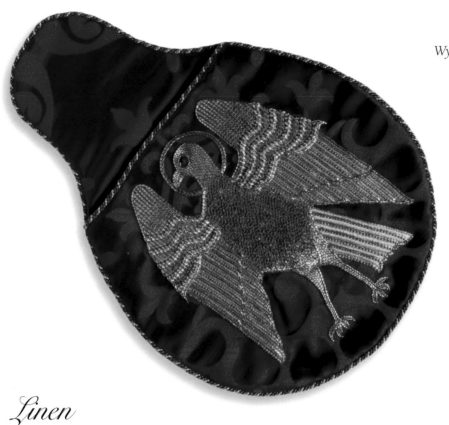

This alms bag was made in Red Wymondham, which enhances the gold embroidery beautifully.

Linen

A solid piece of goldwork covering all the ground, as in the examples on pages 53 and 63, can be worked on a fine linen (or on a heavy calico). When working a very solid piece, as in these examples, you should consider the weight of gold being placed upon the background and choose the appropriate weight of cloth.

Equipment

I always use a **slate frame** for my work. (The word 'slate' comes from the slate used by children before paper was used in schools: when the frame is made up it is the same shape.) Slate frames come in different sizes depending on the work to be undertaken. In the picture opposite is a slate frame made up with a linen base. On it is the working of the project to be found on page 74.

You will also need a **sketchbook** for designing. Get into the habit of putting ideas down in pencil and draw any shapes you delight in. The more drawing you do the more you learn to look, and with a better understanding of shapes (for example, how a flower grows, how the leaves are attached to the stem, how the calyx is set, and how the head petals and stamens lay) the more your embroidery design will become real and alive.

Also required are:

Watercolours, brushes, and coloured pencils: it often helps to add colour to your drawings, but when it comes to designing, colour will be the last decision to be made.

Thimbles: there are two of these. I was trained to wear two thimbles (as you use both hands when working on your frame), one on each of your middle fingers. This helps your needle slide through the fabric and of course protects your fingers!

Felt, string, soft cotton thread, and firm card: used for padding, as shown on pages 42–43.

Embroidery scissors, goldwork scissors and large scissors: for cutting fabrics and threads.

Ruler and tape measure: for measuring accurately.

Marker pens and pencils: for transferring your designs to your fabric.

Masking tape: for attaching your design to the fabric before tracing over it.

Set square or protractor: to enable you to set your fabric straight on the grain, and on your frame.

Strong thread: for sewing linen on to your frame.

Magnifying glass: if needed for detailed work.

PVA glue: for finishing off work.

White tissue paper: for use when sealing work once it has been finished off.

Stiletto: for making holes in linen when making up a frame.

Bees wax: for passing silk thread through when working with gold thread – thread slides through the fabric better, stops knotting and gives the thread strength.

String: for threading the sides of your frame.

Greaseproof paper and tracing paper: used to transfer your design to the fabric, and for making templates for padding, kid and so on. Greaseproof paper is softer and more malleable than tracing paper and therefore preferable when creating templates from three-dimensional shapes.

Design

Design is extremely important, for it is the basis of any good embroidery. I have mentioned on page 18 the importance of learning to 'look'; to be observant and aware. There is so much around us that we don't really look at at all! The natural form in our gardens, the buildings all around us (whether we live in the town or country), the fruit and vegetables we prepare every day, can all be inspirational! It is important to have a sketchbook handy so that you can jot ideas down. Even if you cannot draw easily, take a note of what interests you. The gathering of ideas gives you substance to work upon at a later date. The keeping of a scrapbook can be very valuable too for collecting pictures of things that delight you – from advertisements to photographs in magazines and newspapers.

I often get my ideas flowing by working on a project. I might choose a pile of autumn leaves, for instance. I would start a worksheet, drawing the pile of autumn leaves first; then I would draw the shadow the pile gives; then perhaps another drawing of individual leaves – all very different shapes, with their varied outlines and patterns of veins. By this time I am really understanding the shapes before me – how one line relates to another. I might then draw one leaf beside another and one partly on top of another. I now consider what shape is emerging on the page and whether the drawing (or by now the design) should lie flat on the page or whether the surface should become undulating. Now I would draw a square, an oblong or a circle and place the design which has emerged within one of these shapes, perhaps overlapping the edge of the chosen outline. This would give an entirely different effect, for the background of the shape then becomes important too.

As you will realise, your worksheet will be invaluable for exploring. There are numerous possibilities, and you will find many ideas emerging. I always find it exciting to work in this way for you can never tell what the outcome will be! When you are happy with your design you can then consider colour, which is a vital factor of the whole, and then interpret your design in terms of technique.

Bees' Delight

This design is based on a patio garden. The corners indicate paving while the beaded sections are raised to suggest hedges dividing the main areas. In each 'gravel' section I have placed flowers: convolvulus, antirrhinum, foxgloves and nasturtium. On each pink section I have embroidered vegetables: peas, beans, a courgette and a marrow. All these have flowers that the bees delight in. The calico behind the skep (the beehive) is painted with watercolour, the bees are embroidered, and the skep itself is worked in brick stitch interspersed with lines of cord.

The sampler

I began the sampler, which is the basis for this book, some years ago as a teaching aid. I felt it was the best way for my students to see what techniques were required for the different stitches which they needed to know. They all started to make samplers of their own. In this way they learnt the correct way to make up a slate frame, how to prepare the linen or calico and to set it on the frame, how to stretch and string the frame, and how to attach a piece of fabric before getting on with the stitches. All this information is essential to an embroiderer. The stitches were learnt in easy stages: you will notice that the oblong shape has been used for all the stitches placed around the edge (some narrower than others). This was deliberate as straight lines are essential in goldwork and often much harder to work than curves! Laid stitch needs more space (as it is a filling stitch) than satin stitch, and hence a broader shape. I suggested working two shapes in each stitch, the first to get hold of the idea and the second to get into the rhythm of the stitch, when the working will become a little easier.

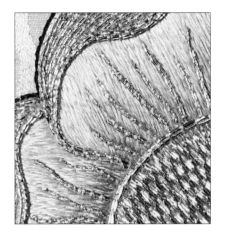

Having made the frame up I suggested that the students plan the shapes on the frame first. Larger shapes were placed at the corners, leaving equal measurements between each rectangle and allowing for a border if one were required. My rectangles were 6cm (2½in) long by 4cm (1½in) wide with 1cm (½in) between each shape. The narrow rectangles measured 6cm (2½in) long by 1cm (½in) wide. At this point we discussed the colouring to be used: this was very important as each person has a real preference for colour. The students were asked to work these essential stitches in the colours they chose and soon the sampler became a very personal piece of work. As the embroidery progressed, so different shapes and designs appeared until in the centre of the sampler the student was asked to work a design of her own choosing using all the techniques learnt on the outside of her frame. These samplers became wonderful references, as well as very personal and beautiful pieces.

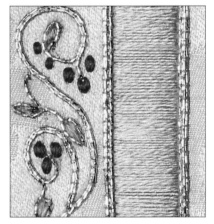

Some years ago I was asked to put on an exhibition of all the samplers worked in and around the Rutland area: they were a wonderful collection and all so different and varied. For me it brought back memories of every single person I had taught. Over the following pages I have described the processes for each stitch I have used, and hope that you might put these techniques into practice and enjoy creating a sampler of your own.

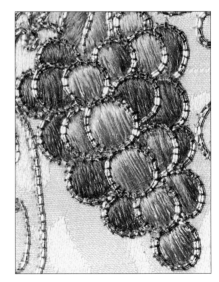

The completed sampler

I worked my sampler on a cream brocade called St Nicholas. Silk of this sort enhances the richness of the piece and gives it lustre.

Getting started

Before you begin, make sure that you have drawn out your design on paper. As well as being a reference for future work, this will enable you to determine the size of the frame you will need, and the size of the background fabric required. As a general rule, you will need 10cm (4in) of spare fabric all around your design, plus 8cm (3in) for turning on the width, plus 2cm (¾in) on the depth.

Preparing the fabric

To determine the width and depth of your linen, you first need to measure the width of your design, adding 10cm (4in) (which will give you space around it) plus 8cm (3in) for turnings (which will give you 4cm (1½in) each side for your slots in which you will place the string). To obtain the depth of your linen, measure the depth of your design and add 10cm (4in) plus 2cm (¾in) for turnings (this will give you 1cm (approximately ½in) at the top and the bottom of the linen). You should now have achieved your correct measurement.

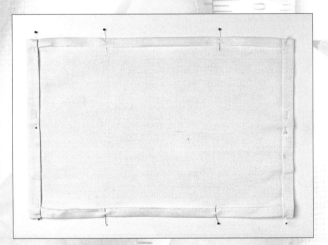

1. Cut out a piece of linen or calico on the grain to the required size. Fold the fabric piece in half lengthways on the grain and mark the centre at the top and bottom of the linen with coloured thread. With the wrong side of the linen facing, turn in the top and bottom edges of the linen (on the grain) 1cm (½in) and pin this fold in place (pin inwards, as the picture shows: this contains the linen better). Turn in each side 4cm (1½in) and fold twice: this double fold makes a slot for the string.

2. Open up each side seam and lay a length of string under the folds. This is to strengthen the sides when they are attached to the frame with string. Machine or back stitch the seams in place.

Framing up

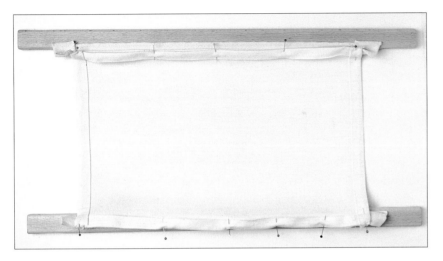

3. Mark the centre of the webbing on both slats with a coloured thread. Pin the top edge of the linen to the webbing at their centre points. Make sure you pull the linen slightly from the centre of the webbing so that you have an even, tight tension. Pin the linen to both ends of the webbing, then pin in between at regular intervals. You will notice that there is 2cm (¾in) of spare webbing on both sides. This is because you need a gap between the edge of the linen and the side of the vertical slat to enable you to pull your string firmly. Pin the bottom edge of the linen to the webbing on the bottom slat in the same way.

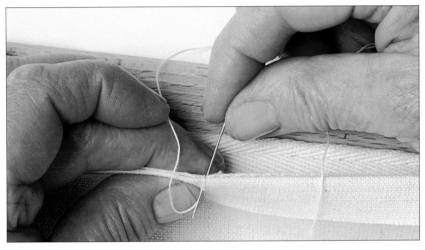

4. Oversew the linen to the webbing at the centre point and then at both ends of the linen (this is because the ends are particularly vulnerable when stringing the frame). Use a No. 8 needle and a strong thread for this purpose.

5. Return to the centre and attach the remaining linen to the webbing using a herringbone stitch. Work to the end, then go to the other side and work a herringbone stitch to the centre. Repeat this process on the bottom webbing.

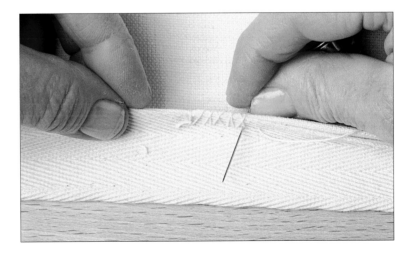

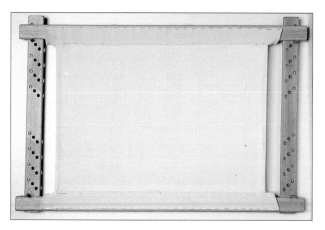

6. Slide in the vertical slats and secure them with the wooden pegs. Ensure the pegs are positioned in the same place on each side of the frame, and that the fabric is held tightly and evenly.

7. You now need to mark the positions of the holes for lacing. Make sure the string is tucked well into the seams while you are doing this. Using a pencil and ruler, make the first mark halfway across one of the side seams, just below the webbing. Make subsequent marks below this one at 2½cm (1in) intervals. Repeat along the other side seam.

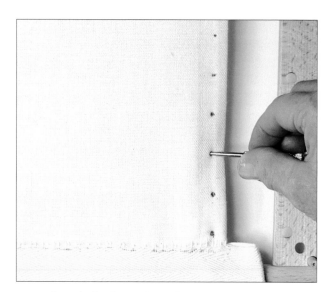

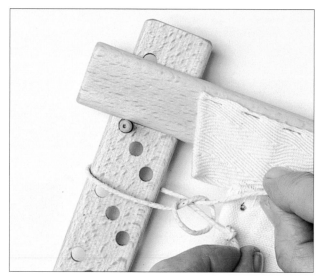

8. Make a hole through each pencil mark using a sharp point such as a stiletto. Be careful not to pierce the string that is tucked inside each seam.

9. Cut off a length of string five times the depth of the linen and make a slip knot in one end. Attach the knotted end of the string around the top left-hand slat and pull up.

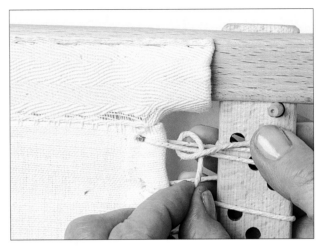

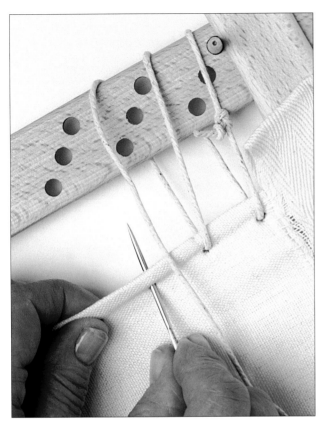

11. Continue weaving the string firmly and evenly along the slat, making sure that the fabric is pulled straight and parallel to the slat. When the first side has been strung, leave it until the second side has been strung, then adjust the tension on both sides so that the spaces on either side of the frame between the linen and the slat are filled equally with string. When you are happy with the tension, wrap the string around the slat twice and secure with a slip knot.

10. Using a large needle such as a tapestry needle, pass the string through the first hole in the linen, from front to back. Then take it behind and back over the slat and pass it through the next hole in the fabric.

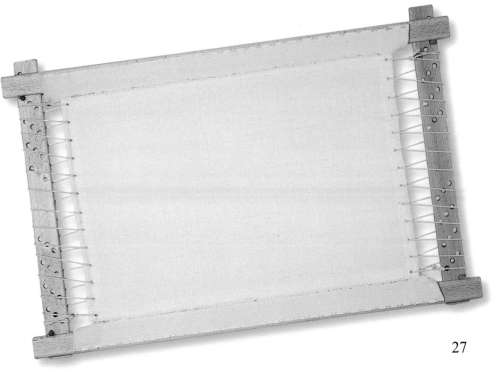

12. You should now have a lovely taut frame which is a delight to work on!

Transferring the design

There are four ways of transferring your design on to the linen base: the light box method, the trace and stitch method, the pounce method and using special carbon paper (which is placed between the tracing and the linen).

The pounce method is one that has been used for many years and is an excellent way of obtaining a perfect replica of your design, though many people now prefer to use either the light box method or trace and stitch, both of which are described below. The pounce method is ideal if no changes are to be made to the design. First take a perfect tracing, then place it on a flat felt base and, with a fine needle (or 'pricker') held perfectly upright, prick around the entire shape making holes at regular (2mm or $\frac{1}{8}$in) intervals. Place the pricking carefully in the right position on your fabric. Hold the tracing paper in position with your hand, or pin the corners of the tracing with needles (which are less likely to mark the fabric than pins), and with a felt roll, rub pounce powder all over the lines of the design. Remove the tracing paper carefully, making sure you don't smudge the pounced lines, then mix an even amount of watercolour paint on a palette and use a fine watercolour brush to paint the lines with a continuous stroke. Use black or white paint according to the background colour. Pounce powder is made in two colours – black and white – and is obtainable from art shops.

Light box method

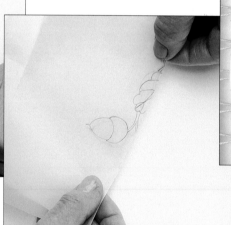

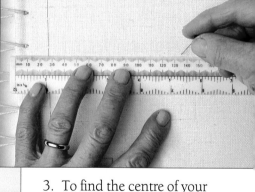

1. Begin by tracing your design on to tracing paper. Always take two tracings – one to transfer on to your background fabric and one to keep as a reference.

2. Fold your tracing in half horizontally and vertically to obtain the centre of your design.

3. To find the centre of your background linen, first lay a ruler squarely across the top half of the linen and mark the centre point with a pin.

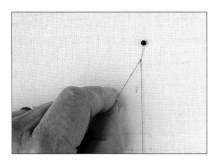

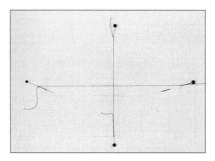

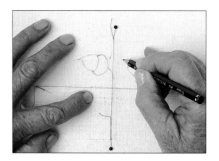

4. Tie a contrasting thread around the pin.

5. Follow the same procedure at the bottom of the linen, securing the thread around the lower pin. Measure and mark a centre line across the width of the fabric in the same way. With a protractor, check that your two threads are absolutely straight.

6. Attach your design to the back of the linen using masking tape. Align the fold lines on the tracing with the threads marking the centre of the linen. Working on a light box, trace over the design using an HB or B pencil or a marker pen.

Tracing method

This method involves using top stitching to mark the design. Some people are happy to retain the surface stitching and embroider over it. However, if you prefer, use a sharp-pointed pencil to draw a fine line by the stitches on to the fabric so that the impression is there. The stitches can then be removed.

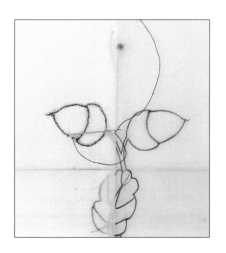

1. Place the tracing of the design on top of the linen and align it with the centre lines as before. If you need to hold the tracing in position, pin the corners of the tracing using fine needles (these will not mark the fabric). Use a small back stitch to sew around the outline of the design using a No. 9 embroidery needle and ordinary sewing cotton. Use the same coloured thread as you intend to use for your embroidery so that you can sew over it if necessary.

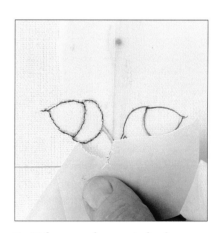

2. When you have stitched around the whole design, carefully tear off the tracing leaving the surface stitching behind. Begin by tearing around the outside of the design and then remove the paper left within the shapes.

Beginning a thread

Start by tying a small knot at the end of your thread. Bring the thread up close to where you wish to begin sewing but where it will be covered by subsequent work. Take the needle back through the fabric to form a tiny securing stitch, then bring it back up ready to start your embroidery.

When laying stitches that will later be removed, leave the knot at the start of the thread on the top of the fabric. To remove the stitches you then simply have to snip off the knot and lift them out.

Beginning a thread.

Ending a thread

Pass the thread up through the fabric close to where you finished sewing but where it will eventually be hidden underneath your embroidery. Take the needle back through, forming a single, small stitch. Bring the needle back up and cut off the thread. Always cut off the thread on the top surface of your fabric.

Forming the finishing stitch.

Cutting off the thread.

Passing through a gold thread

Always use a chenille needle for passing a gold thread through fabric. Place the needle vertically halfway through the fabric as shown. Thread it with the gold thread, then pull the thread through the fabric. Leave a tail of about 1cm (½in) on the back of the fabric.

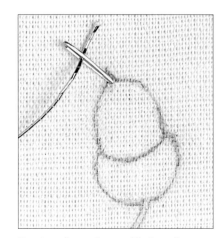

Passing through a gold thread.

Autumn

This piece forms part of a series of trees, each depicting a different season. The tree is padded slightly in the middle to give it a raised appearance, and the apples are worked in a felt-padded satin stitch using a terracotta floss. The leaves are cut from felt in various shades of orange, yellow and red, and the background is painted calico. The garden, which is different in each picture, has tufted threads depicting grass, and apples which have fallen to the ground.

Winter

By kind permission of Mr and Mrs Julian Amey.

The tree is worked on a calico background that has been painted using watercolour. The trunk is raised slightly in the middle, as in Autumn. The trunk and the branches are worked in brick stitch, and where the moon's rays rest, a silver thread has been added.

Spring

This tree is worked in exactly the same way as Winter and Autumn, but to indicate
Spring I have created blossom using beads in various shades of pink, and leaves
cut from green felt.

Stitches

On the following pages I have described all of the embroidery and goldwork stitches that I have used on my sampler. All have been worked on a linen ground, and for teaching purposes worked into simple shapes, though I have occasionally included a small project in the form of a design to consolidate what you have learnt, and to give you the opportunity of applying your knowledge in a more interesting and creative way. At the end of the book I have included an acorn project to show you how different colours and stitches can be combined in different ways, and the beautiful effects that can be achieved using the techniques you have learnt in the preceding sections.

Goldwork is a beautiful art form, and one which requires a high level of skill and concentration, but the satisfaction that can be gained from mastering the skills involved and producing designs of your own is enormous. As my background is in ecclesiastical embroidery, I use a combination of goldwork and silk embroidery, the coloured silks complementing and enhancing the richness of the gold. Raised embroidery, worked over a padding, is a wonderful way of giving your work a three-dimensional feel and really makes the gold threads shine out. I have therefore included a section on padding, and have worked a number of stitches over a raised base.

As you progress with your work, it is important to realise the need to pass gold threads through the fabric as you work (see page 30). Never pass the threads all together when you have finished the piece in hand, for you will have missed the opportunity to make a beautiful shape with your gold thread. On page 47, for example, there is a leaf worked in satin and laid stitch. You will see clearly that the gold threads have been passed one at a time at the top and bottom of the leaf, and dovetailed. The result is a beautifully shaped leaf with a sharp point.

This attention to detail is essential throughout your work – always keep the shapes of your stitches neat and consistent, and when working in straight lines, keep your lines evenly spaced and parallel. Take time to practise the techniques and perfect them – they will equip you with everything you need to know to design and produce a piece of work of your own, and to try out the numerous gold threads, coloured silks and background fabrics that are available.

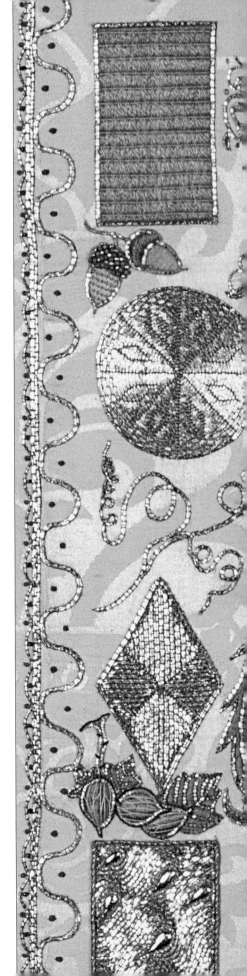

Laid stitch

Laid stitch is a very old form of embroidery. It is used as a filling stitch and considered a far quicker form of embroidery than long and short stitch (see pages 48–49). In the past, if a client commissioned a banner of a certain design and found the cost of working it too high, the embroiderer would have to interpret the drawing and use quicker methods to make it, perhaps using appliqué or stitches that would fill larger areas more quickly. This is when laid stitch would come into its own!

Laid stitch is a surface stitch, as its name implies. The first stitch is worked from the top of the required shape to the bottom, and the next stitch from the bottom to the top, with no gap in between. This procedure continues until the shape is filled. Always use a substantial thread for this purpose: a floss is ideal. I usually work with 46cm (18in) lengths of floss – any longer and the floss becomes worn with use. In my example I have used two threads together so that the linen is well covered.

Having finished this first stage you will see that these long stitches would be completely useless and would catch with the slightest touch, so the tying-down stitch is essential and is worked to complete the whole. This tying-down stitch is worked from the left side of the shape to the right, with the sewing thread travelling under the surface of the linen (see step 2). The silk used for tying down can vary in thickness but I have used a fine silk thread in a contrasting colour.

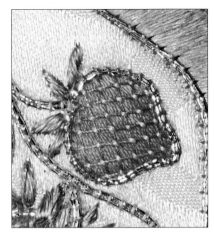

The strawberries on the sampler are worked in laid stitch couched down with lattice threads and with a yellow stitch placed on every crossed line.

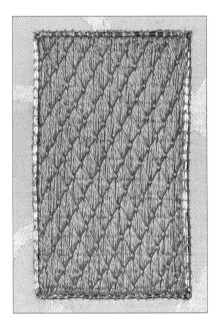

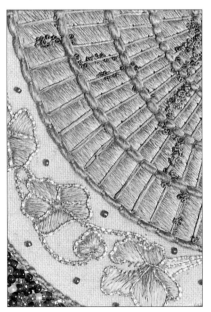

The rectangle shown far left is taken from the sampler. It is worked in laid stitch that has been couched down with trellis stitch, and given a gold border.

The detail on the left is from Bees' Delight (see page 21). The laid stitch is tied down at intervals to give an impression of garden tiles. The 'gravel' area is painted with watercolour, and beads have been sewn around the nasturtium, which is worked in orange-yellow silk floss and surrounded with gold thread.

36

Begin by drawing out a rectangular shape on the linen. The rectangle should measure 5 x 2.5cm (2 x 1in).

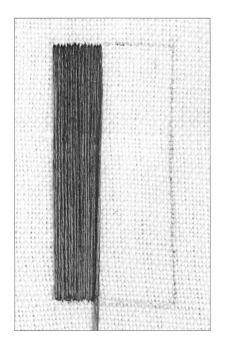

1. Using two threads of silk floss and a No. 8 sharps needle, start with a knot and small stitch to secure the threads. Bring your needle up at the top left-hand corner of the rectangle. Create the first stitch by taking the needle down through the fabric at the bottom left-hand corner, ensuring that the thread lies perfectly parallel to the vertical edge. Bring the needle up as close as possible to the first stitch and continue laying even, close stitches until the shape is filled.

Tip
When filling a shape with a solid area of embroidery, always take the needle to the outer edge of the shape, so that the pencil outline is hidden beneath the embroidery.

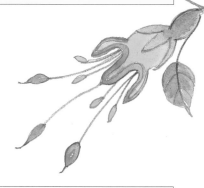

2. Change to a No. 9 sharps needle and a fine silk thread, and lay parallel tying-down stitches going from left to right across the shape, approximately 3mm ($^1/_8$in) apart. Lay the first stitch along the top edge of the rectangle, and work down to the bottom edge, with the thread travelling beneath the linen.

Tip
To achieve a neater finish, lay a silk thread in the same colour as your embroidery along the top and bottom edges. This is illustrated in Step 2.

3. Using the same needle and thread, use brick stitch (see pages 50–53) to secure the tying-down threads. Take each stitch just above the tying-down thread and just below it, keeping the stitches as small and as neat as possible. Leave approximately 3mm ($^1/_8$in) between stitches. Start at the top left-hand corner of the rectangle and work down to the bottom right.

Couching

Couching is a means of stitching gold threads to a background fabric using a different thread. In this case I am using imitation Jap gold to surround the rectangle on page 37 and a pure silk thread for the couching.

Traditionally, gold threads are couched down in pairs as this gives a finished and more substantial look. It will also enable you to pass the two threads at slightly different points at the corner to obtain a good shape. The procedure for turning corners is shown on pages 39–40. I always try to work either one or both of the gold threads from the reel, rather than cutting off lengths as required. This is a more economical method of working, and the threads are less likely to be damaged.

The distance between the couching stitches depends upon the style and texture you wish to achieve in your finished design. It is important always to keep your stitches straight and even, firm but not so tight that they pinch the gold.

Couching stitches are usually worked at right angles to the gold thread, but if you need to place a diagonal stitch when turning a corner, make sure you hold the silk firmly beneath the frame, then keep the gold threads taut while you turn them to form a really sharp bend. (See steps 3 and 4 opposite.) Always twist the gold thread slightly as you work to ensure that the core of the thread remains evenly covered. You would do this if you were using real Jap gold as well.

A section taken from the sampler showing gold threads couched down using coloured silks. On the left, long and short stitch (see page 48) has been worked in floss and covered with a trellis of metallic thread. The shapes within the rectangle on the right are filled with satin stitch worked over card.

1. Cut a length of gold thread that is long enough to go round the perimeter of the rectangle, plus an additional 1cm (½ in). Thread a chenille needle with the gold thread and pass it through the fabric at a point just above the top of the rectangle so that it lies adjacent to the left edge of the shape. Pass a second gold thread through just to the left of the first thread and at a point just above it. Keep this thread on the reel. There is no need to secure the threads at the back of the embroidery, as they will be held in place by the couching.

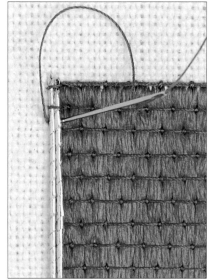

2. Using contrasting silk thread and a No. 9 sharps needle, couch down the two gold threads. Remember to keep your couching stitches straight and evenly spaced. Hold down the gold threads firmly while you work. Remember to twist them slightly as you work so that the core of the gold does not show.

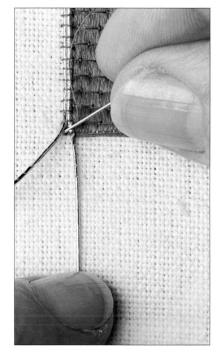

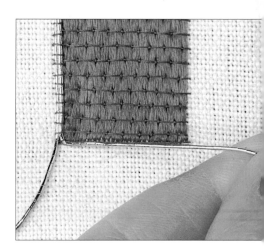

3. When you reach the first corner, hold the inner gold thread taut and secure it with a small diagonal stitch, worked from right to left.

4. To ensure a sharp corner, turn the inner gold thread tightly back on itself.

5. Lay the inner gold thread along the horizontal edge of the rectangle.

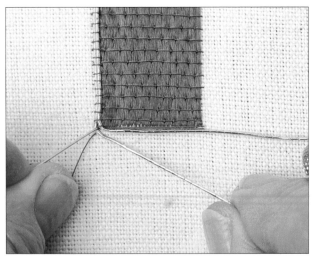

6. Secure the corner of the outer gold thread with a small diagonal stitch, worked from the outside edge to the inside. Hold the thread taut while you make the stitch, in the direction in which it will be laid.

7. Lay the two gold threads together along the bottom edge of the rectangle. Hold them taut and make sure the corner is sharp and square. Couch down the two gold threads.

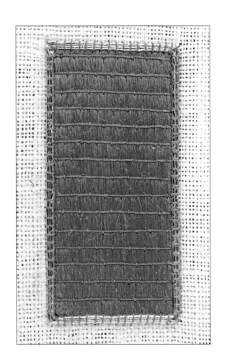

8. Continue round the rectangle and complete the couched edging by passing the two gold threads back through the fabric at the point where they started (the top left-hand corner), making sure that they 'dovetail'. Finish off by couching down each gold thread separately at the corner using a diagonal stitch. First secure the inner gold thread working from the inside outwards, and then secure the outer gold thread working from the outside in.

Trellis stitch

This is an alternative, more decorative tying-down stitch and an easier one to work, although it doesn't look it! Here I have shown the process of working the stitch in its simplest form, but when used within an embroidery it can be embellished with beads or gold threads. It is important that the stitches are evenly spaced.

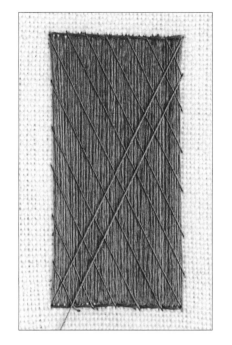

1. Using contrasting silk thread and a No. 9 sharps needle, begin in the top left-hand corner of the rectangle, and take the first tying-down stitch across diagonally to the bottom right-hand corner. Take the thread back up beneath the linen, and repeat. Complete all the stitches going in this direction, filling first one side of the rectangle and then the other, before starting those going in the other direction. Keep the stitches parallel and evenly spaced by placing the thread in the correct position and holding it taut while you make each stitch.

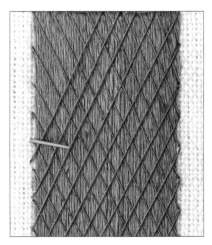

2. Continue to build up the trellis pattern, passing the needle through the same holes as the previous stitches to ensure a neat finish to your work.

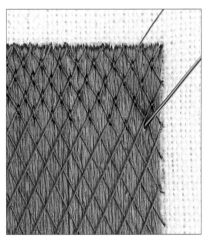

3. Using the same needle and thread, lay small securing stitches at the intersections of the diagonal threads. Keep these as small, neat and even as possible.

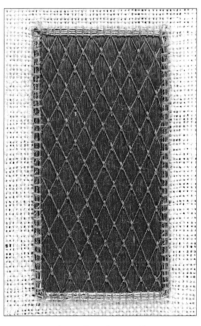

4. Complete the design by couching down a gold border (see pages 39–40).

Padding

You can introduce different levels to your design by working parts of it over a padded base. Adding depth in this way gives a beautifully rich, textured feel to your work. Four different types of padding can be used, each producing a very different effect. The floss and cotton paddings shown below give a more rounded finish, whereas the card padding shown on the facing page produces a sharper edge. Floss gives a finer padding than cotton.

Felt padding should be used if you require more height than can be achieved with a stitched or card padding. It also gives a more rounded finished to your embroidery. Here I have described felt padding with only two layers, but if you require more height to your design you can add more layers as needed. Planning the height of your work before you start is important so that you can graduate the felt (always place the largest piece on top).

Floss padding

This type of padding is made using long stitches running the length of the shape you wish to fill. Use two strands of silk floss, and alternate long and shorter stitches. Leave a narrow 2mm (⅛in) unpadded border around the edge of the design to give a smoothly rounded shape to the finished piece.

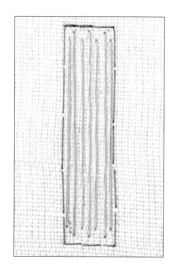

Tip
When using a stitched padding, always make sure that the padding is sewn in the opposite direction to your embroidery stitch or gold threads.

Floss padding.

Cotton padding

This is created in the same way as floss padding, but using thick, soft padding cotton. It gives a more raised effect.

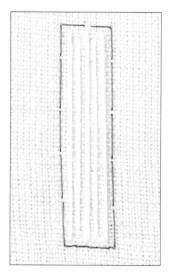

Cotton padding.

Card padding

Card padding is used when a sharper edge is needed. The card is cut to fit just within the shape and tied down in place with large slanting stitches worked across the card. Smaller stitches are then worked at a slant around the edge, bringing the needle up through the fabric and taking it down through the card. A No. 8 needle and a fine thread are used.

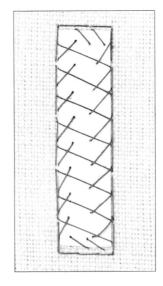

Tip
Always pass the needle down into the card when sewing; never bring it up through, as this is more likely to cause damage.

Card padding.

Felt padding

To pad a rectangular shape with two layers of felt, begin by cutting out the first layer of felt, approximately 2mm ($^1/_8$in) smaller all round than the shape you wish to pad. Secure it using stab stitches placed along its length.

Cut out the second layer of felt, this time approximately 1mm ($^1/_{16}$in) smaller all round than the shape. This ensures that it fits comfortably over the first layer, and lies just within the shape you wish to pad. Hold the felt in position using diagonal holding stitches (shown far right). Finally, stitch it into place around the edge using slanting stitches. These are less likely to damage the felt than stitches placed at right angles to the edge as these may cut into it. Always come up with your needle through the fabric and go down into your felt – never come up into your felt as this could easily displace it.

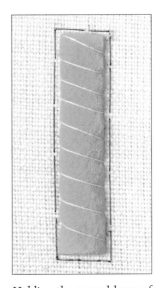

Securing the first layer of felt using stab stitches.

Holding the second layer of felt in position using diagonal holding stitches.

To pad a circular shape, follow a similar technique. Hold the second layer of felt in position using long stitches that cross in the centre of the circle, like the spokes of a wheel, and secure the felt using slanting stitches placed around the edge.

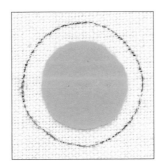

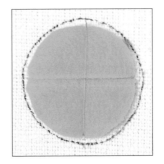

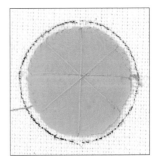

Padding a circle.

Satin stitch

Satin stitch is a very beautiful stitch, enhancing any embroidery and giving it lustre. It is nearly always worked over a padding to lift it from the background (see pages 42–43). The stitch itself is a continuous one worked from one side of the shape to the other. Go over the surface of the padding with your thread and back underneath the fabric so that your needle comes up on the same side of your shape every time. This gives the stitch a tautness which will enhance the floss and, when the floss is stroked, give a wonderful lustre to your work. To stroke the floss, lay a chenille needle across the surface of the floss and stroke it firmly (not using the point of the needle). This helps the threads lay evenly, and gives them a beautiful sheen.

Satin stitch cannot be used to fill very wide areas as the surface would not remain taut and the floss would wear. You will see below that I have used a floss padding: this is ideal if you do not need too much height. You would use a felt padding for more height and a card padding if a sharp edge were needed.

Begin by drawing a rectangle measuring 1 x 5cm (½ x 2in) and filling it with floss padding in the same colour as the satin stitch (see page 42).

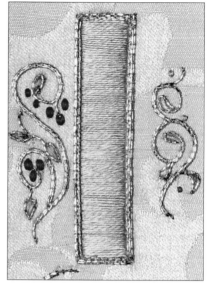

A detail from the sampler, showing satin stitch worked over a floss padding.

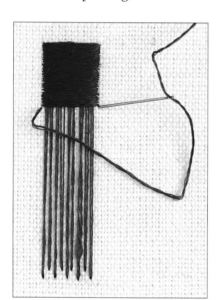
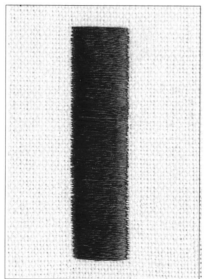

1. Using a 46cm (18in) length of thread, create the first stitch by bringing the needle up through the fabric in the top left-hand corner of the shape, and taking it back down on the other side. Make sure the stitch runs parallel to the top edge of the shape. Make the next stitch by bringing the needle back up just below the start of the first stitch, and as close as possible to it. Take the thread across the shape so that it runs parallel to the first stitch. The two stitches should be as close as possible to each other without overlapping and with no gap between the two. Continue down until the shape is completely filled.

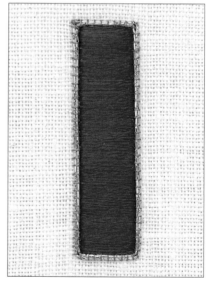

2. To complete the design, add a gold border (see pages 39–40) couched down using a silk thread in a contrasting colour to the satin stitch.

This panel is taken from my sampler. I have worked the vine leaves using two tones of green floss; the larger leaf is worked in darker tones than the smaller leaf. Both leaves are slightly padded with a floss padding (see page 42). The veins and leaf outlines are worked in K5 Jap gold thread and couched with green silk thread.

The grapes down the centre of the bunch are each padded with a tiny felt circle, while those at the back are padded with floss. This gives more height in the centre of the bunch, and therefore a feeling of roundness to the whole. The grapes are worked vertically in satin stitch using a single thread of silk floss and then surrounded individually with two threads of K5 Jap gold, working from the back of the bunch forwards. For the tendrils I used K5 Jap gold, remembering to pass one thread above the other at the tip to obtain a good shape.

Decorative leaf design

This project is to encourage you to put into practice the stitches learnt in the previous sections (pages 36–45). Here laid stitch and satin stitch have been put together to form a leaf shape. I have worked the leaf in two different coloured flosses, but in step 3 I have used a variegated cotton thread to show the effect it can give.

You will need a No. 8 sharps or embroidery needle, soft cotton thread for padding, silk floss for embroidering, K2 imitation gold thread for the surrounding edge and silk thread for couching down.

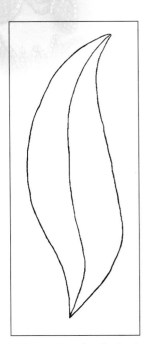

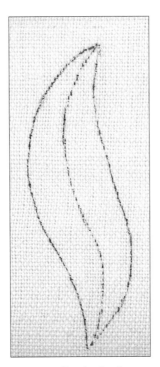

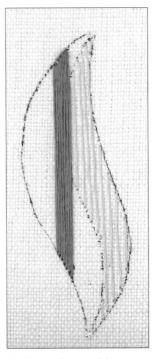

The template for the leaf design, reproduced actual size.

1. Transfer the leaf design on to the fabric using one of the methods described on pages 28–29.

2. Begin by padding the right-hand side of the leaf with long, vertical stitches. In this case I have used a soft cotton padding thread (see page 43). When completed, fill the left-hand side of the leaf with laid stitch worked in dark green floss (see page 37).

Tip

When filling a shape with vertical stitches, in this case with either laid stitch or cotton padding, begin by placing the first stitch down the centre of the shape. Work from here outwards to one side, then return to the centre and work outwards to the other side. This helps to keep your stitches straight and parallel.

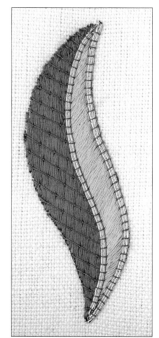

4. Complete both sides of the leaf, securing the tying-down stitches on the left-hand side using small stitches (see page 37). Couch down two gold threads to form the central vein, first passing through the two threads, the outer one above the inner, at the top of the leaf (see page 39). Work down the vein with couching stitches until you reach the bottom of the leaf and then pass through one thread above the other to finish off.

Surround the leaf with gold thread, working one side at a time. Pass the gold threads through at the top, placing the inner thread lower than the outer thread to form a point. Work down the outside of the leaf with couching stitches, taking your needle from the outside into your work. When you reach the bottom of the leaf pass through the inner gold thread first to the back of the work, and then pass through the outer thread at a slightly higher position. To outline the other side of your leaf, place the gold threads in between those already there when passing them through top and bottom. This is called dovetailing, and will make a beautiful shape.

3. Lay tying-down stitches diagonally across the laid stitch on the left-hand side of the leaf using a No. 9 sharps needle and silk thread in a matching colour. These stitches imitate the veins of the leaf. Fill the right-hand side with satin stitch, mirroring the angle of the tying-down stitches on the left (see page 44). Here I have used a variegated cotton thread to show the effect that can be achieved.

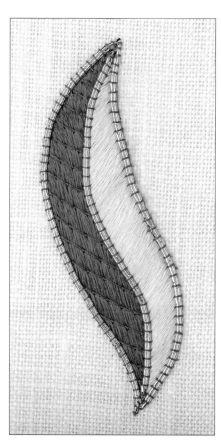

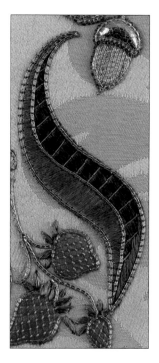

A detail from my sampler, showing a leaf worked in a similar design.

The finished leaf surrounded with gold thread.

Long and short stitch

This is an ancient form of embroidery stitch, one that is extremely beautiful to look at but can be difficult to achieve. It is a filling stitch and can be used with different thicknesses of silk embroidery thread. In ecclesiastical embroidery it is a stitch that is 'split' when worked (which means that the needle pierces the thread when it comes up into the floss). It is also a stitch that goes back upon itself a little in the second and subsequent rows: this ensures the work is well covered, and when only one colour is used gives a wonderful richness and sheen. As you become more accomplished, you should use either a single thread of floss, or two threads of fine twisted silk. When shading is needed, different tones of the same colour can be incorporated. The size of the needle varies with the thickness of the thread, but usually a No. 9 sharps needle is used. The first and most important thing to remember is that after the first row of long and short has been completed all the stitches in the subsequent rows are the same length. It is only the lengths of the stitches in the first row that give the stitch its name!

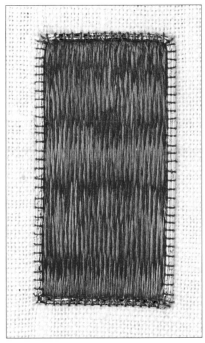

This rectangle is worked in two shades of colour so that the positions of the stitches can be seen clearly, and to show how two similar colours can merge.

The rose at the centre of my sampler is worked in long and short stitch using a paler colour towards the outside than at the centre of the flower. On to this I have worked rays of fine gold thread.

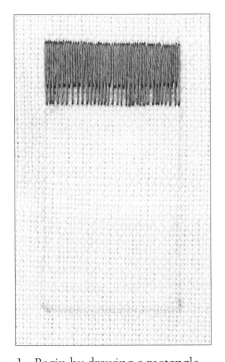

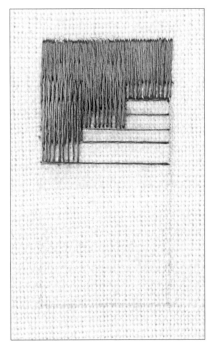

1. Begin by drawing a rectangle on to your linen. It should measure 2.5 x 5cm (1 x 2in). Using one thread of floss and a No. 9 sharps needle begin by sewing the first long stitch in the top left-hand corner of the rectangle. The length of the stitch depends on the size of the shape to be filled, but in this case it should be approximately 1.5cm (¾in) in length. Bring the needle back through at the top of the rectangle as close as possible to the first stitch and lay the second stitch, which is the short stitch. The length of this stitch should be slightly more than half the length of the long stitch. Lay alternate long and short stitches until the first row is completed.

2. To illustrate the second row clearly I have used a contrasting colour. Place your needle underneath the linen and bring it up through the first long stitch just above the end of the short stitch in the previous row. Take your needle down into the linen making this stitch the same length as a long stitch in the previous row (1.5cm or ¾in). Start the second stitch 0.5cm (¼in) below the top edge of the shape and bring your needle up through the first short stitch of the first row. Make this stitch the same length as the first stitch, so that it ends just below the long stitch in the first row. Repeat this process until the second row of stitching is completed.

3. Work the third row (shown here in the same colour as the first row) following the same method as the second row. I have placed straight horizontal lines in this picture to show the positioning of the stitches more clearly.

Tip
Remember that each stitch you work splits the stitch in the previous row, and after the first row all the stitches are the same length.

49

Brick stitch

Brick stitch is a surface stitch: this means that the gold threads (which are always worked in pairs) lie on top of the fabric and are held down by couching stitches worked in a finer silk thread. The couching stitches are sewn in the form of bricks in a wall, hence the name brick stitch. It was the first stitch I learnt at the School of Embroidery and one that it was important to master as it is the crux of all good goldwork embroidery. It is essential to work brick stitch carefully, making sure that the stitches are straight and evenly spaced. Colour and pattern can be introduced into your design by working the couching in one or two contrasting colours. This can be seen particularly well in the project on page 58.

Brick stitch can be used to fill large areas very satisfactorily. When the gold threads are passed through the fabric, there is no need to secure them at the back of your work as they will be held in place by the couching stitches. Make sure, though, that they are not lying over your work, otherwise they may become entangled in subsequent stitching. If necessary, turn them away from the work and hold them in place. When a section is finished, turn the frame over and cut off all the gold ends, leaving a tail approximately 1cm (½in) long.

Over the years, the ways of using gold thread have changed a little, although the fundamental method of working it has not. At one time the gold would have been worked across the design (as in Or Nué) and the depth of shadow and fullness of folds would have been achieved by closeness of the stitchery. Later, the gold thread would have been worked vertically following the lines and shapes of the folds, so more movement became apparent (as in the Cope Hood shown on page 11). Nowadays we use gold thread in both these ways, each giving different but wonderful effects.

By working gold threads across the design, as in Or Nué, you are dependent upon the positioning of the stitches to give different depths to the work. When working around a shape, as in the example on page 53, you can allow the gold thread to lay more freely. This seems a more natural way of working with this wonderfully malleable thread, and I just love the freedom that it can give.

Both these ways of working with gold are exciting, and when you have a design that can be interpreted in so many different ways, then that is when you can begin to take a real delight in your work.

I used brick stitch to embroider the outer parts of the rose petals on my sampler.

Tulips

This piece is worked in Or Nué. It is an advanced form of embroidery and takes a very long time to work! First your design is painted on to the calico, and the gold threads (always two threads together) are then worked from the bottom to the top. To start off, they are passed one above the other on the right-hand side of the design and laid across it. No. 9 sharps needles are then threaded, each with a different coloured thread as dictated by the design, and brick stitch worked from right to left, changing the thread colour accordingly. When the end of the first and each subsequent row is reached, on the left-hand side, the two gold threads are passed through to the back of the fabric. The next row is then started just above the previous one with no gap in between the two.

51

Turning and passing

The example below uses a method called 'turning and passing'. It enables the embroiderer to fill a shape without passing in both threads at the top and bottom every time.

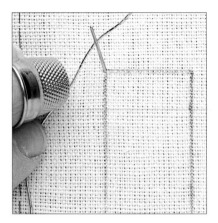

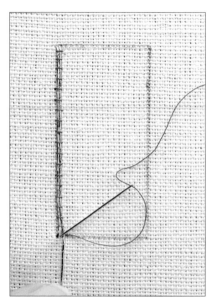

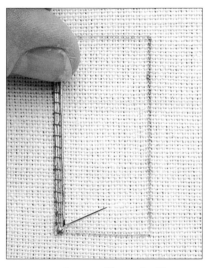

1. Begin by marking out the shape you wish to fill on your fabric: in this case a rectangle measuring 5 x 2.5cm (2 x 1in). Pass the first gold thread through the fabric in the top left-hand corner of the shape. Cut off the length required for the first line of gold, equal to the depth of the rectangle (5cm or 2in) plus an additional 1cm (½in) for passing through.

2. Pass a second gold thread to the right of the first, keeping this thread on the reel. Couch down the two threads all the way to the bottom left-hand corner, working the stitches from right to left (this ensures that no space is formed in between the pairs of threads). As you work, keep the second gold thread taut and hold it as close as possible to the first gold thread to create an even line. Pass the first thread in at the corner, and take a stitch over the second gold thread to secure it at the bottom.

3. Bring the needle up halfway, just to the right of the second gold thread, and turn this thread sharply upwards to form the third line of gold thread.

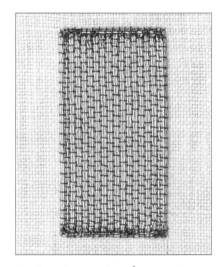

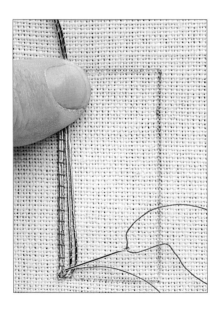

4. Cut off the gold thread from the reel, ensuring it is as long as the rectangle plus 1cm (½in). Pass a fourth gold thread at the bottom of the rectangle next to the third, leaving it attached to the reel. Couch down these last two threads.

5. Continue using the turning and passing method, working your way up and down the shape until all of it is filled. Couch a gold border around the rectangle to finish (see pages 39–40).

Golden Eternity

By kind permission of Mrs Innes Bullard.

This is a very advanced piece and is worked entirely in gold thread with small sections of kid. The curved shapes have been worked first, starting with the centre shape, and brick stitch used in the inner sections. This is a wonderful example of the sense of fluidity and movement that can be achieved using gold threads.

Golden diamond design

In this project, you will be using brick stitch in a more interesting and decorative manner. I devised this diamond shape to teach my students how to make sharp corners. I have used a K3 imitation Jap gold thread, and a No. 9 sharps needle and a red silk thread for the couching to make the stitchery clearer.

There is quite a lot to think about when working this shape; not only are there the corners to consider, but also the passing in of the two gold threads has to be very sharp on both the horizontal and vertical lines and also on the edge of each segment. The turning and passing method, described on page 52, is not appropriate to this shape, or indeed any shape that requires a very sharp outline – this can only be achieved by passing both threads through each time. At the corners, each gold thread has to be stitched separately to form a sharp bend. This is explained in the following instructions.

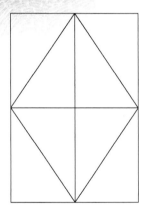

The template for the diamond design, reproduced actual size.

Tip
When working with pairs of gold threads, remember to cut one to the correct length, allowing 1cm (½in) for passing through, and leave the other attached to the reel.

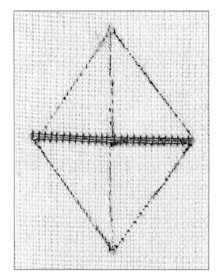

1. First transfer the design on to the background fabric using the template (see pages 28–29). On the right-hand side, pass two gold threads either side of the centre line running horizontally. Starting on the right, couch down the two threads, taking the stitches from above the gold threads to below them. When you reach the left-hand edge of the shape, pass the two gold threads through.

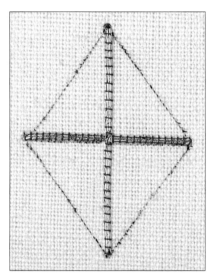

2. Pass two gold threads through at the top point of the diamond, one either side of the centre line, and couch them down to the bottom point. Make sure one gold thread is placed either side of the centre line. The vertical line is more important than the horizontal in this design, which is why it must be worked over the top. Pass the gold threads in at the bottom.

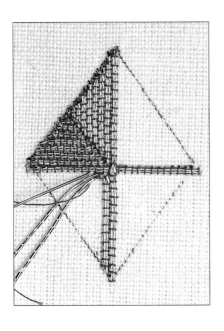

3. Fill in each segment of the diamond with L-shaped lines. Begin by passing through two gold threads on the sloping line (the outline), exactly next to the vertical line, and couching to the centre. Work the stitches from the outside into the shape. At the centre, turn the inner gold thread sharply (as explained on page 39), and place a couching stitch worked from the outside into the corner at an angle. Turn the second thread in the same way. Continue couching, keeping the needle on the outside of the gold as you come up so that there is no gap created between the gold threads. Pass the two threads in through the fabric on the sloping line.

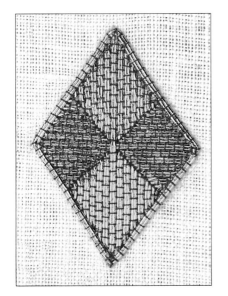

4. Complete the diamond by couching a gold border around the outside edge of the shape (see pages 39–40). Notice how the variation in the colour of the gold thread is achieved by the direction of the threads, adding depth and richness to the design.

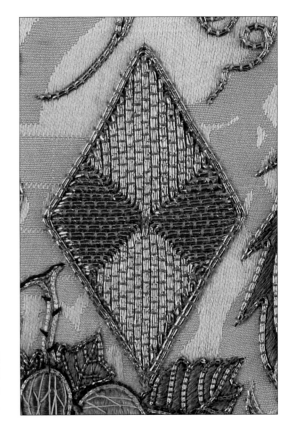

The diamond design, couched using green silk, on my sampler.

Golden circle design

There are so many ways of using gold, and in this project I am laying the threads on the surface of the fabric in order to make a circular form. It shows very clearly the malleability of the gold thread. I have embellished the circle with simple, straight lines of couching in a contrasting colour. A more intricate design worked within the same shape is also shown.

For working gold into a circular shape it is best to use a fine thread (K4 imitation Jap gold is ideal) as a thick thread would not turn so well. I use a silk thread for couching down the gold, and a No. 9 sharps needle.

First draw a circle measuring 4.5cm (1¾in) diameter on to your fabric. Using a pencil or marker pen, draw within this shape eight diagonal lines, as shown in step 1. If a sharper line is required, these can be tacked in, as shown in the first two steps.

Gold will not sit neatly around a curve without being held in position with a stitch. You will see, therefore, when you arrive at step 4 that more lines have been drawn in between those already worked to mark the positions of the additional stitches required as the circle widens.

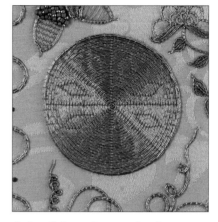

A detail from the sampler showing surface stitch worked in a circle. The securing stitches have been worked in a pattern using silk thread in a contrasting colour.

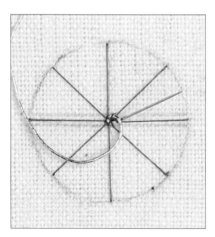

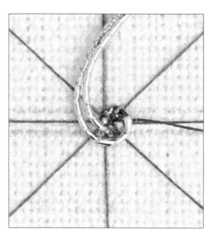

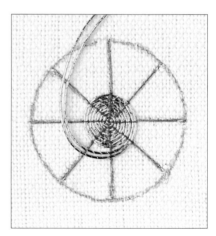

1. Pass through a single gold thread at the centre of the circle. Keep this thread on the reel. Secure it with a small stitch placed on one of the diagonals. Curve the gold thread round to form a tight inner circle, positioning the securing stitches so that they lie on the diagonals.

2. Continue round once more, and then pass through a second gold thread, just inside the first. This second gold thread should be cut from the reel and must be long enough to finish the whole shape (to pass a new thread at any point within the circle would be very difficult to hide).

3. Continue forming the circle, placing securing stitches over the two threads on the four diagonals to create the pattern. Work the securing stitches from the outside in towards the centre of the circle. This helps keep the circle as neat and tight as possible.

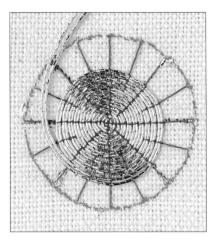

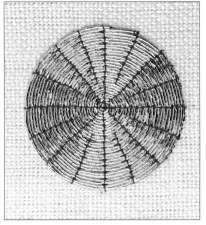

The completed circle.

Tip
Be firm with your gold threads – place them exactly where you want them to go, and remember to always work the securing stitches from the outside in towards the centre of the shape. This helps to hold the circle together and to maintain a regular shape.

4. When you have worked approximately one-third of the circle, draw in four more diagonals, halfway between the first, and place securing stitches on these also.

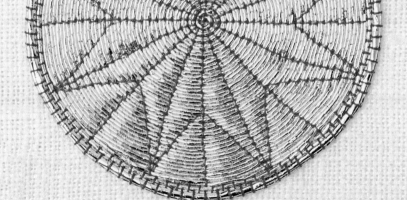

This circle has a more decorative finish, created by placing securing stitches in a pattern. For the gold border, pass the inside thread first, just within the worked shape, and the second thread, offset slightly, just outside it. Work around the circumference of the circle, sewing equally spaced couching stitches, and taking the needle from the outside and working inwards to ensure the edge of the work is completely covered and to create a perfect circle. When you arrive at the point where the two outline threads meet, pass the inside thread first and then the outer thread, dovetailing the two ends together in each case.

Diamond design using two colours

In this project I have used brick stitch (see page 50) couched down in two different colours to fill a rectangle with two diamond shapes drawn in the centre. It shows clearly how designs can be created by simply changing the colour of the couching thread, and the angle at which the stitches are laid – those lying on the diamonds' edges are worked at an angle relative to the gold thread, producing the two green outlines.

Begin by transferring the design on to your fabric.

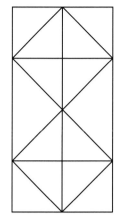

The template for the design, reproduced actual size.

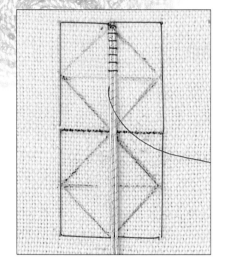

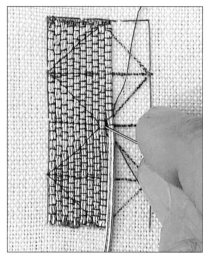

1. Pass through a length of gold thread at the top of the rectangle just to the left of the centre line. Cut off the thread leaving a tail 2cm (¾in) longer than the rectangle. Pass through a second gold thread to the right of the first. Leave this thread attached to the reel. Couch down the two gold threads using a red silk sewing thread. When you reach the bottom of the shape, cut off the right-hand thread leaving a 2cm (¾in) tail and pass both threads through.

2. Pass two gold threads at the top of the rectangle, just to the left of the first two, and complete the left-hand side of the shape. Work the right-hand side in the same way, from the centre line outwards. Couch down the gold using red and green stitches, according to the pattern of the finished design. Outline the diamonds by working the stitches at an angle, following the outlines of the shapes. On the horizontal lines, lay stitches side by side to create a solid line. Keep the red and green threads on separate needles as you work, and always work from the outside of the shape into the centre.

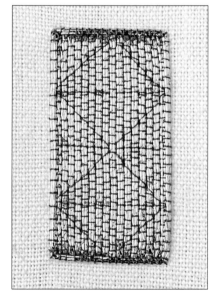

The finished embroidery, with a couched gold border.

Golden Circle

This design has been worked on a green silk background. The top layer of the shape is decorative, using gold thread and cords over string, while the bottom layer, the inner part, is worked in curved brick stitch using a terracotta silk thread for couching.

Kid

Introducing kid into your design will help give it a wonderful liveliness, though in my opinion it should be used sparingly and thoughtfully: it can look inartistic when used in slabs. Kid should always be used so that it merges into the design and it is nearly always padded. The area to be filled with kid should always be worked with a solid area of goldwork around it so that the finished design looks well balanced.

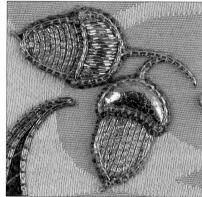

The acorns on my sampler are worked in brick stitch. The cups have been worked in raised gold and kid.

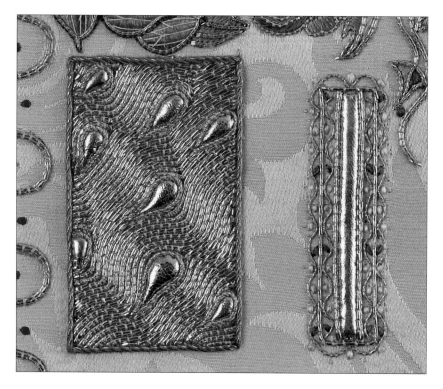

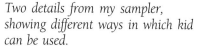

Two details from my sampler, showing different ways in which kid can be used.

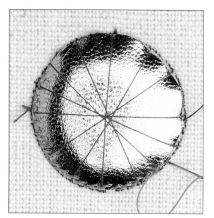

1. Begin by drawing a circle measuring 4cm (1½in) in diameter on to your linen, and adding two layers of felt padding following the technique shown on page 43. To achieve the right sized circle of kid, place a piece of greaseproof paper (it is softer than tracing paper) over the two thicknesses of felt and pencil around the shape. This will allow for the fullness of the felt. Place the greaseproof template on to the wrong side of the kid and draw around the shape. Cut it out using sharp scissors on the pencil line. Secure the kid over the felt by using long tacking stitches that cross the shape like the spokes of a wheel. These long stitches should be done with a fine silk thread as this will not mark the kid as would a thicker thread. Sew around the edge of the kid using slanting stitches taken from the outside and going down into the kid. Use a fine No. 10 sharps needle and a silk thread. This is a vulnerable edge, so your slanting stitches should wrap the edge and not pull it.

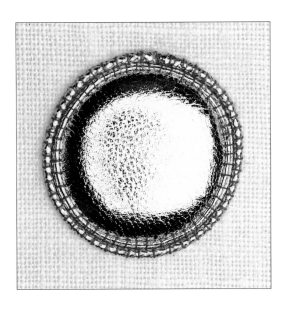

2. Once the kid is sewn securely to the background, remove the tying-down stitches and complete the design with a gold border. In this case, two pairs of gold threads have been couched down using brick stitch. (See page 57 for instructions on adding a border to a circle.)

Tips

Slanting stitches are used to edge fragile materials such as felt and kid. This is because they 'bind' the edge and do not cut into it, as might shorter stitches placed at right angles to the edge.

Always sew downwards into kid, not up through it – this gives you more control over the positioning of the stitches, and is less likely to cause damage to the kid as you pass the needle through.

To add kid to an oblong shape, first draw an oblong on to your fabric – the one shown here measures 1.5 x 6.5cm (¾ x 2½in). Add two layers of felt padding following the technique shown on page 43.

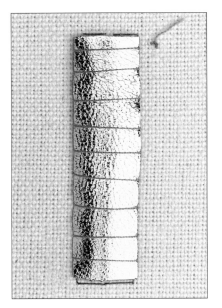

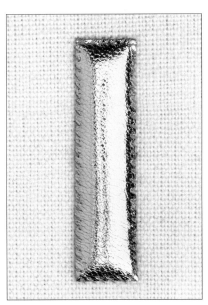

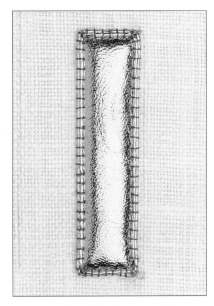

1. Secure the kid over the two layers of felt padding using long, parallel tying-down stitches.

2. Sew the kid in place with a fine needle using slanting stitches, then remove the tying-down stitches. Do not leave in the tying-down stitches longer than necessary, as they can mark the kid.

3. Complete the shape with two threads of gold couched down around the edge (see pages 39–40).

Three circles design

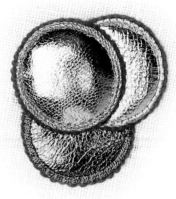

These three overlapping circles were created using three templates – one complete circle shape and two shapes cut from the circle, one slightly larger than the other. No felt padding was needed under the bronze shape as it is placed at the back of the other two shapes. One layer of felt padding was placed under the silver kid as this is lying on top of the bronze, and two pieces of felt padding (one smaller piece of felt placed under the top piece) were placed under the gold kid as this is on top.

   The gold and bronze circles were given a gold border (see page 57), and the silver circle was given a border worked in silver thread. Matching silk threads were used for the couching stitches. Each circle was then surrounded with six strands of fine embroidery silk to finish, couched down using red silk thread. Notice that the circle at the back (bronze) should be surrounded first, followed by the silver and then the gold. Use a No. 9 or 10 sharps needle for sewing into the kid.

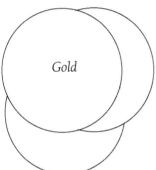

Gold

Bronze

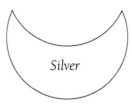

Silver

The templates for the design, reproduced actual size.

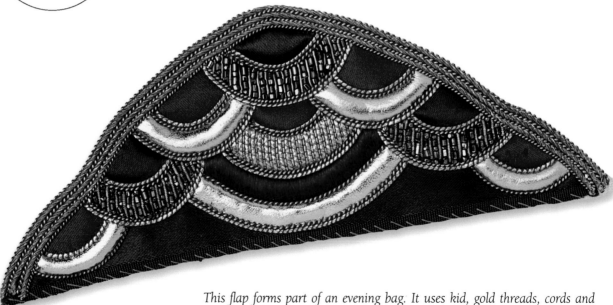

This flap forms part of an evening bag. It uses kid, gold threads, cords and purple beads worked on a purple satin background.

Morning Star

By kind permission of Mrs Innes Bullard.

In this design the central shape has been padded to give a raised
effect and worked using cords, threads and beads. The sections in
between have then been worked in brick stitch and kid. I have
used different coloured silks and close stitching within these
sections to create intense tones.

Decorative lozenge design

To obtain different textures in your work you need to be able to incorporate different materials and stitches. This small project uses gold kid and brick stitch together, using K3 imitation Jap gold.

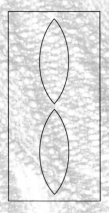

The template for the lozenge design, reproduced actual size.

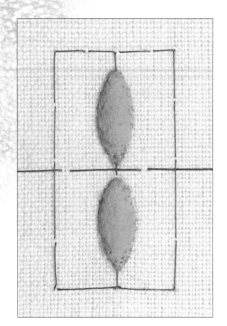

1. Begin by transferring the shape on to your background fabric. Add two layers of felt to each lozenge shape following the method described on page 43.

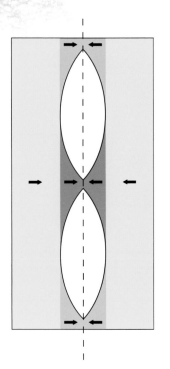

Stage 1

Stage 2

Stage 3

2. Attach a layer of kid to each lozenge shape (see pages 60–61) and fill in the background using brick stitch (see page 52). Use a No. 8 sharps needle and K3 imitation Jap gold thread. Start the background brick stitch in the top left-hand corner of the oblong, passing in two gold threads at this point (Stage 1 in the diagram shown on the left). Couch down the two gold threads working from the outside of the oblong in. When you reach the bottom of the shape, pass the two threads back through. Go back to the top of the oblong and pass two more threads next to the first two. Couch them down, this time working from the inside out (this ensures that there are no gaps between the gold threads). Continue to fill the left-hand side of the oblong area with brick stitch, until you reach the edge of the lozenges. Repeat this procedure on the right-hand side of the rectangle.

Having worked both sides, return to the centre section and fill in the areas left around the lozenges. Go back to the top edge on the left-hand side of the space to be filled and pass in two threads (Stage 2 in the diagram). Work down to the edge of the lozenge and pass in the threads, one above the other. Go back to the top edge and work to the centre (your lines will become shorter as the lozenge shape goes to a point). Work the right-hand side of the gap in the same way, then repeat the process in the space left at the bottom of the shape.

Now fill the space left in the middle of the shape (Stage 3). Pass two threads in at the edge of the top lozenge on the left-hand side, work down to the edge of the bottom lozenge and pass the two threads in one behind the other. Pass two more threads next to the first row and work down, this time passing the left-hand thread in on the edge of the bottom lozenge and turning the other gold thread upwards. Take a stitch in the loop, and turn the gold thread back down at the base of the top lozenge. (Make a securing stitch to hold the loop of gold in position.) Now sew the two turned threads together. Continue in this way until you reach the centre. Work the right-hand side in the same way. (By turning the two threads and sewing over them you are achieving the same effect as passing the threads, which in such a small area would be very difficult to do.)

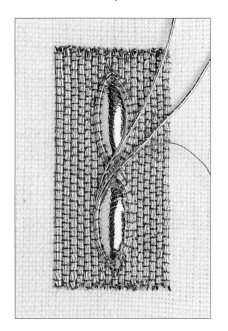

3. You are now ready to finish the design by outlining the two lozenges in the form of a figure eight. Pass two threads, one slightly beyond the other, on the left-hand side of the top lozenge, and work around the two shapes. Bring the couching threads up on the outside of the gold threads and work down into the kid. To make a sharp point at the tip of each lozenge, take a stitch over the inside thread first and then the outside stitch, working them in a straight line. Turn the gold threads sharply as you work around the point.

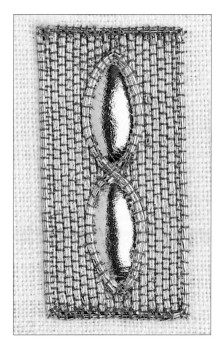

The completed design.

Teardrops design

This small, more advanced project is an excellent way to gain valuable practice in working with kid and gold thread in a more fluid way. One of the beauties of goldwork is the sense of movement and freedom that can be gained from working the gold threads into gentle curves and shapes. The changing patterns of shadow and light that this creates can be truly breathtaking.

The kid used here is fairly light in weight, and the colour works well with the K3 imitation Jap gold chosen. The teardrop shapes are very small, so it is better to use only a single layer of felt for padding. When one layer of felt is used it is important that a good shape is cut with sharp scissors (making sure it is a little smaller than the shape drawn on your linen), and that it is secured to the background by tacking it in position first and then sewing around the edge as explained on page 43.

Use a No. 9 sharps needle for sewing the kid, and a No. 8 or 9 for the brick stitch. For the couching, use a fine silk thread in a contrasting colour.

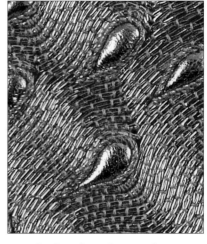

Detail taken from the sampler.

The template for the teardrop design, reproduced actual size.

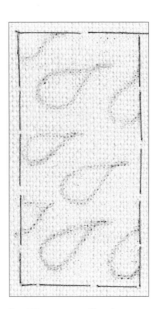

1. First, transfer the design to your background fabric and outline the rectangle using tacking stitches to give it a sharp defining edge.

2. Add a single layer of felt padding to each teardrop, secured using small, slanting stitches (see page 43).

3. Attach a layer of kid to each teardrop. Sew it on carefully, ensuring that the stitches are sufficiently slanted to avoid them cutting into and damaging the edges.

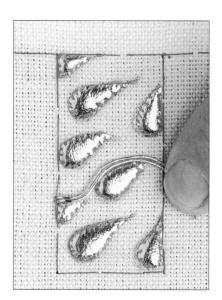

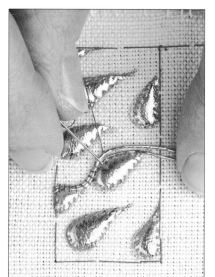

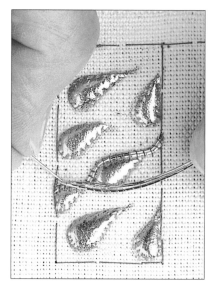

4. Starting in the centre of the design, build up the background by laying lines of gold couched in pairs across the shape, working them closely around the teardrops.

5. The first line of gold is important as it defines the shape of the subsequent ones. Hold the two gold threads firmly in position while you couch them down, working the stitches from the outside in. It is important that you actually attach the couching to the kid to obtain a snug fit around the teardrops.

6. At the end of the line pass the two gold threads back through the fabric. Start the second line of gold, which will lie adjacent to the first line and just above it.

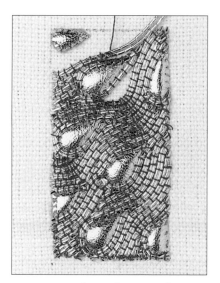

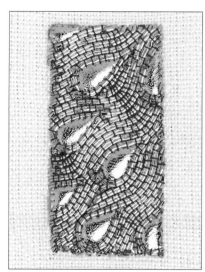

7. Work the third row just below the first one. Gradually build up the background by moving outwards from the central line.

8. Remove the tacking stitches and continue building up the background. Fill any small spaces left in the background at the end.

The completed design.

Raised gold

Raised gold involves laying gold threads over a raised surface. It is a wonderful form of embroidery for it can bring so much light to any design. The thickness of padding can vary according to the depth required in your design, but the width of raised gold cannot exceed 1cm (¾in) – if wider than this, the gold would become worn and the threads would not stay firmly in place. Here I have used K4 imitation Jap gold, and a No. 9 sharps needle for the couching.

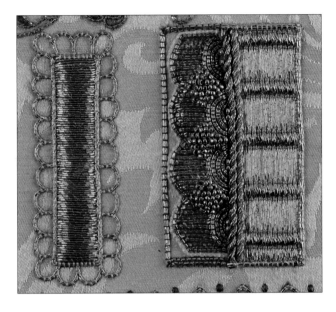

Two details from the sampler, showing raised gold worked over felt on the left-hand side, and raised gold worked over string on the right-hand side of the oblong on the right.

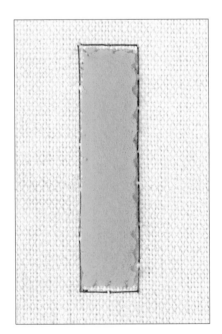

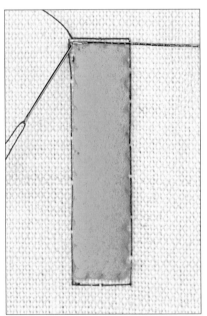

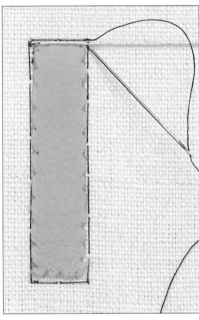

1. Transfer the outline of the shape on to your fabric, using either a pencil line or tacking stitches (as I have here). Build up two layers of felt padding, as described on page 43.

2. Working straight from the reel, pass a single gold thread through the top left-hand corner of the shape. Hold the thread firmly in place across the top of the felt and harness the thread using a single couching stitch, worked from top to bottom.

3. With the thread across the felt, (allowing for the fullness of the raised shape), from the top right-hand corner take a tiny stitch over the gold thread. Make sure the gold thread is lying parallel with the edge of the rectangle, and as close as possible to it.

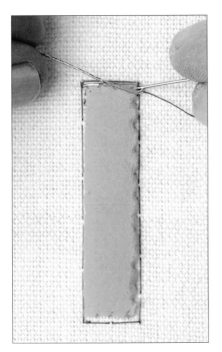

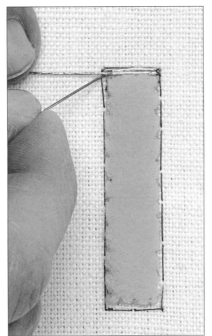

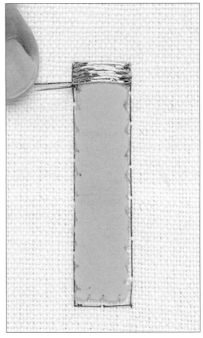

4. Turn the gold thread sharply around your needle, and harness it on the bend with a tiny stitch placed snugly beside the first. Take a tiny securing stitch by the edge of the felt to secure it.

5. Lay the gold thread back across the shape. Take your needle across the back of the work and bring it up on the left-hand side. Keeping the gold thread as close as possible to the one above, take a stitch over the gold thread (worked from bottom to top) and turn the gold sharply. Sew a securing stitch by the edge of the felt.

6. Continue working backwards and forwards across the shape, keeping the gold threads as straight and as close to each other as possible, and allowing for the fullness of the felt. Work each stitch from bottom to top, and harness each one with a small holding stitch placed just below it by the edge of the felt.

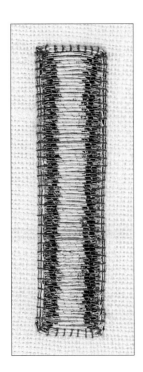

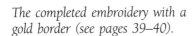

The completed embroidery with a gold border (see pages 39–40).

Tip
You may get a small gap between the first two threads where they lie over the edge of the felt. This can easily be adjusted later.

Basket stitch

Basket stitch is a surface stitch that can give height and texture to any goldwork design. It is worked over string, which can vary in thickness according to the thickness of the gold thread used. I have used a white-coloured string but very often gold-coloured string is used for this purpose. The thickness of string used opposite is suitable for use with K3 imitation Jap gold.

Basket stitch can be worked with alternate gold threads, as I have used in the centre of the rose on my sampler. Here I have used a fine K5 Jap gold thread. In the worked example on pages 71–73 I have used three pairs of gold threads (remembering that it is always correct to work gold threads in pairs).

It is very important when using this stitch that the foundation is worked extremely carefully – the string must be placed evenly on the background, and each piece of string must be carefully shaped and sewn firmly in position – for the gold basket work will not stay in place if not.

Detail from the sampler, showing the centre of the rose worked in basket stitch using alternate threads of K5 Jap gold.

Details taken from the sampler, showing basket stitch worked into two rectangles. The left-hand shape has been worked with two pairs of K4 Jap gold threads in each section (remembering that you always use two threads together), and the right-hand shape has been worked using three pairs of K3 Jap gold threads per section.

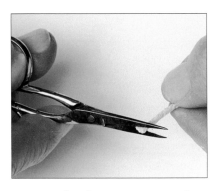

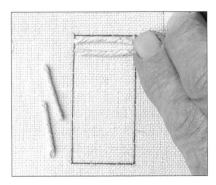

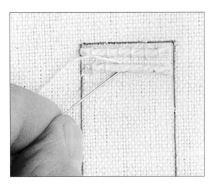

1. Begin by drawing a rectangle measuring 2.5 x 5cm (1 x 2in) on to your background fabric. Cut lengths of string measured accurately to fit just within the outlined shape: in this case just under 2.5cm (1in). Twelve pieces will be required. Trim the ends of the string at an angle to create a smooth edge.

2. Lay the string across the shape, placing it just within outline. Space out the string evenly leaving gaps between the strings equal to the width of string, and make sure that the cut edge is facing upwards.

3. Attach each piece of string to the fabric using matching thread and evenly spaced overstitches. Pass the needle up through the fabric at a slant from underneath the string, take the thread over the string, and pass the needle back through at a slant on the other side. This closeness of stitch to the string will ensure a firm hold.

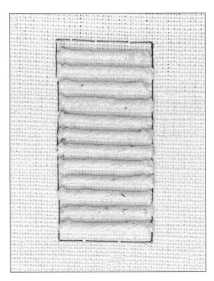

The rectangle with all the string in place.

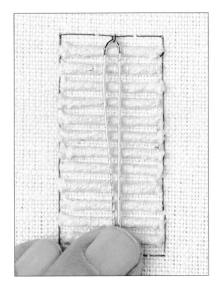

Tip
As you sew, hold the string in place with a pin if necessary, but be careful not to break the twist of the string.

4. Starting in the centre at the top of the shape, make a loop in the gold thread and harness it to the fabric with a single stitch worked from the edge of the shape in. Leave the right-hand thread attached to the reel; the left-hand thread should be twice the length of the rectangle plus 2cm (¾in).

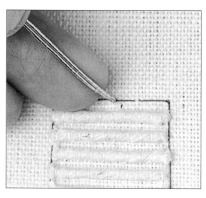

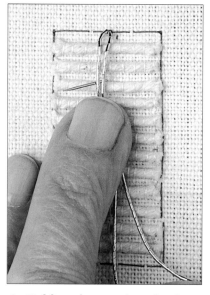

5. Place a small holding stitch just within the shape. Pull the gold threads back firmly whilst holding the sewing thread tightly underneath the frame. This helps to straighten the gold thread in readiness for laying it down in position on the linen.

6. Holding the two threads of gold in place, bring the needle up at a slight angle from underneath the gold threads and just to their left, and between the second and third pieces of string.

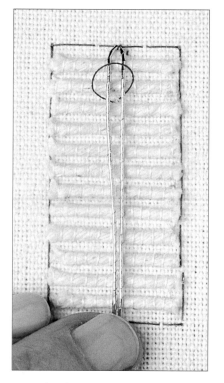

7. Take the needle back down on the other side of the gold threads, again at a slight angle, to form a stitch. Take another tiny stitch by the side of this stitch to harness it. Make sure that the gold thread is raised slightly over the string to give the embroidery depth. If you pull the gold too tightly it will lie too flat and the three-dimensional quality of the work will be lost.

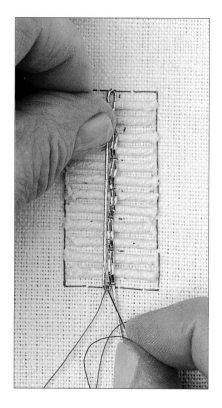

8. Continue to the bottom of the shape, then turn the left-hand gold thread sharply upwards (see page 52). Bring your needle up through the linen and take a stitch over the thread at the base of the turn.

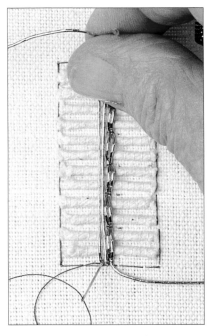
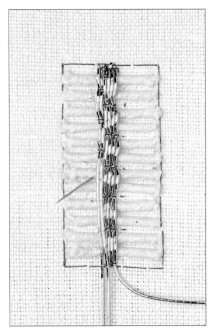
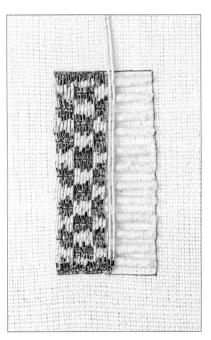

9. Cut the gold thread from the reel, leaving a tail equal to the length of the rectangle plus an extra 2cm (¾in). Working again from the reel, pass a gold thread exactly next to the turned thread and work your way back up the shape, placing your couching stitches as in the first row.

10. At the top of the rectangle, pass the right-hand gold thread through and turn the left-hand thread down sharply. Cut this thread from the reel as before, and pass through another gold thread next to the previous one, again working from the reel. Couch down the two left-hand threads, this time placing your stitches between the first and second strings, the third and fourth strings and so on, thus creating the basket weave effect.

11. Complete the left-hand side of the rectangle, changing the position of the securing stitches every third pair of gold threads. Start the right-hand side of the shape at the bottom, turning the thread left on the reel at the start of the first line of gold, and passing through a second gold thread just to its right. Place the securing stitches for these first two gold threads in the same positions as those just to their left. Change the positions of the securing stitches every sixth line, as before.

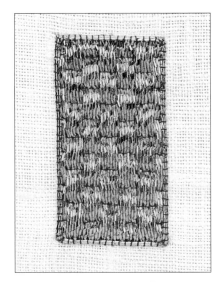

The completed design, with a gold border.

Tip
Always work your securing stitches from the outside of the design inwards. This helps to draw the gold threads together.

Acorn project

I have always been inspired by natural form, and the acorn seems to lend itself perfectly to interpretation using a number of the techniques I have described in this book. I have drawn a small design which you should be able to complete fairly quickly, and have worked it twice, using different techniques in each case.

By working through these two projects, you will consolidate much of what you have learnt in this book, and in the process I hope you will gain the inspiration and confidence to move forward with your goldwork and create designs of your own.

For each project you will need Nos. 8, 9 or 10 embroidery needles and a chenille needle. The materials required are listed separately under each project.

Template for the design, shown actual size.

74

Design 1

In this design I have worked the acorns predominantly in gold. For the brick stitch on the two nuts, the raised gold on the right-hand cup and the veining on the leaf I have used K4 imitation Jap gold thread, and for the gold border around the acorns and leaf and for the stems I have used K3 imitation Jap gold. All the couching is worked using gold-coloured sewing silk, though I have used green in the example below so that the stitching is clearer. The leaf is filled using laid stitch worked in a variegated green floss. A small piece of felt is required for padding the acorn cups, and greaseproof paper for covering the raised felt in preparation for cutting the kid. The finished acorns and stems have been edged with a light green silk floss couched down with green sewing silk.

In both this and the following design, the stems have been given a raised edge by working two layers of couched gold threads. Having laid and couched down the first two threads, lay another pair over the first, placing one thread on top of them down the centre of the stem and the second alongside them, just to the left of the left-hand thread. Couch down the second pair by working the stitches from the outer edge inwards, passing the needle back through the fabric in between the first two threads laid.

The completed embroidery, shown actual size.

The nuts

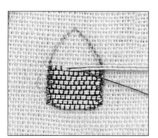

1. Starting at the base of the shape, work the right-hand acorn in brick stitch using the K4 imitation Jap gold thread. Lay the gold threads horizontally, passing the first two one above the other on the left-hand edge of the nut. Continue up the nut, passing the threads in at the sides to retain a good shape. Make sure that your couching stitches are worked from the top to the bottom of the gold threads so that there are no gaps between the rows. Add a gold border to finish.

> **Tip**
> Because the nut is slightly rounded I have worked the first row beginning and ending the gold threads within the nut shape.

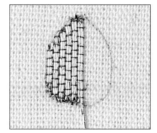
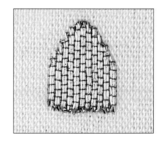

2. Create the left-hand acorn also using brick stitch, but working vertically with the threads. Always start in the centre of the shape and work outwards, first to the left and then to the right.

The leaf

The leaf is worked in laid stitch using two shades of green floss. Combining two different shades of green creates an interesting variegated effect. Twist together two strands of silk floss as you work. When you transfer your design, draw in the curving central vein to divide your leaf in two.

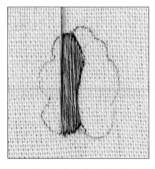

1. Place the first laid stitch down the centre of the left-hand side of the leaf, and work first towards the vein on the right, and then towards the left.

2. Complete the right-hand side in a similar fashion, working first towards the vein and then towards the right.

The completed laid stitch.

3. Couch down two gold threads for each vein, and complete the leaf with a central vein, stem and border couched down using green silk thread.

The cups

1. Begin by applying three layers of felt padding to each cup as shown. The sizes of the pads need to be made progressively larger to achieve a smooth, domed shape.

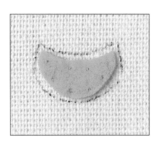

The first layer of felt, stab stitched in place.

The second layer of felt, stab stitched in place.

The third layer of felt, secured with slanting stitches worked around the edge.

2. You now need to measure the fullness of the left-hand cup so that when the kid is cut it is the correct size. Place a small piece of greaseproof paper over the felt shape, and draw around it with a marker pen or pencil. Cut this shape out with sharp scissors and tie it down over the felt to see that it fits perfectly. Release the paper shape and place it on the wrong side of the kid. Mark around the shape with a marker pen or pencil and cut this out with sharp scissors. Now you have a perfectly shaped piece of kid to cover the raised felt.

3. Tie the kid in position with a fine silk thread (this will not mark the kid as would a thicker thread), then sew around the edge of the kid using a silk thread and a fine needle. Remember to use slanting stitches worked from the outside of the shape into the kid (never come up with your needle into the kid). Remove the positioning threads.

4. Complete the right-hand cup using raised gold over the felt padding. Start at the top in the middle as this helps you maintain a good, symmetrical shape. Take a loop of gold thread over the shape and make a stitch over the gold loop at the bottom, working from right to left, using a fine silk thread in a matching colour. Let the single gold thread lie with some fullness over the felt shape. Harness with a tiny stitch just under the felt shape so that it doesn't show. Turn the gold thread up firmly, laying it over the raised felt. Continue to fill the right-hand side of the shape, turning the gold on each edge of the shape and working the securing stitches from the outside in. Pass the gold thread in at the point and with a firm stitch secure the end. Repeat this process on the left-hand side of the cup.

When you have completed both the acorns, add a gold border first to the cups and then the nuts, turning a single gold thread up at the top of the nut to finish.

Design 2

This design is a mirror image of Design 1. I have worked the right-hand nut in laid stitch using a light green silk floss with a decorative lattice tying-down stitch worked in gold sewing silk. The cup is worked with variegated green beads sewn over a felt-padded base. The left-hand nut is worked in vertical satin stitch (for which I used the same light green floss) over a silk padding, and the cup is worked in variegated fine green ribbon which is tied down over a felt-padded base (this is worked following the same method as raised gold). For the leaf I have used the same method as for Design 1. The gold outline, the veining on the leaf and the stems are all worked using K3 imitation Jap gold.

Attaching beads

Beads are always sewn securely using a waxed thread, and it is often advisable to use a fine bead needle as the eye of an ordinary sewing needle may not be small enough to allow the beads to pass over easily. Beads can be used singly, as in borders like the one on my sampler, but very often they are used in groups to achieve some lovely textural effects.

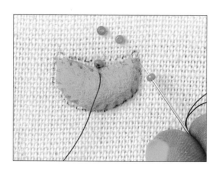

1. To sew on the beads, thread a fine needle with a length of waxed thread. Knot the end of the thread and pass it through to the front of the fabric. Pick up a bead with the point of your needle and push it down to the end of the thread. Secure the bead with a single small stitch, taking the needle through the fabric at a slight angle underneath the bead. If the hole is big enough, take a second stitch through it. Bring the needle back up through the felt leaving a small space just large enough for the next bead.

2. Secure the second bead adjacent to the first and continue in this manner until the shape is filled.

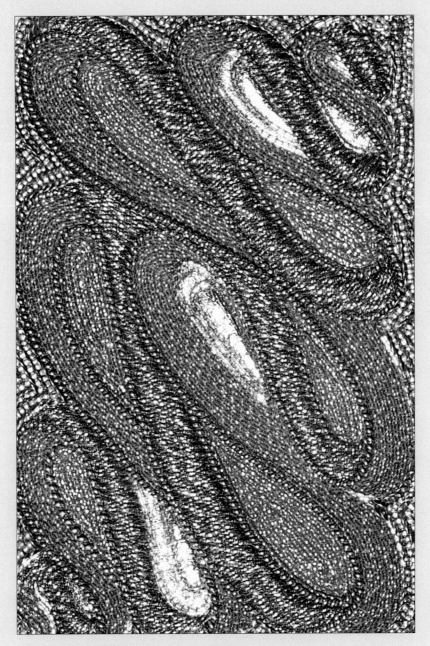

Movement

This is a detail taken from a design worked in tones of blue-green to indicate the movement of the sea. Having decided which areas of the design were to be padded, I started working from the centre outwards, taking the threads around the shapes to achieve a sense of fluidity. Beads and sequins have been added to give a tactile effect.

Index

basket stitch 70–73

beads 13, 21, 33, 36, 41, 62, 63, 78, 79

borders 13, 22, 38–40, 47, 55, 57, 61, 62, 75

brick stitch 10, 21, 32, 36, 37, 50–53, 54, 58, 59, 60, 61, 63, 64, 66, 75, 76,

circles 43, 56–57, 60–61, 62

colour 10, 14, 22, 34, 48, 50, 58

coloured threads 14, 34
    silk floss 10, 14, 36, 44, 46, 48, 75, 76, 78
    silk thread 8, 14, 36, 38, 45, 46, 50, 54, 56, 59, 62, 66, 75, 77, 78
    twisted embroidery silks 14, 48

Comper, Sir Ninian 6, 8, 10

cords 12, 21, 59, 62, 6,

couching 14, 38–41, 47, 50, 52, 54, 56, 58, 64, 66, 67, 75

design 10, 18, 20–21, 22, 24, 34, 50

diamonds 54–55, 58

fabric 16–17, 24, 34

filling stitch 22, 36, 48

frames 15, 18, 22, 24

framing up 22, 25–27

gold threads 12–13, 34, 38, 41, 50, 56, 66, 68, 70
    imitation Jap gold 12, 13, 38, 46, 54, 56, 64, 66, 70, 75, 76, 78
    Jap gold 10, 12, 13, 38

kid 15, 60–61, 62–63, 64–65, 66–67, 75, 77

laid stitch 22, 34, 36–37, 46, 75, 76, 78

long and short stitch 10, 36, 38, 48–49

metallic threads 13

needles 15, 18

Or Nué 50, 51

padding 10, 18, 34, 42–43, 44, 68
    card padding 38, 42, 43, 44
    cotton padding 42, 46
    felt padding 31, 43, 44, 45, 60, 61, 62, 64, 66, 68–69, 75, 77, 78
    floss padding 42, 44, 45, 78

passing through (of gold threads) 15, 30, 34, 38, 54, 55

raised gold 60, 68–69, 75, 77, 78

satin stitch 10, 22, 31, 34, 38, 44–45, 46, 47, 78

silk embroidery 6, 34

silver threads 12, 13, 32, 62

storage (of gold threads) 13

surface stitch 36, 50, 70

transferring designs 18, 28–30

trellis stitch 41

turning and passing 52, 54, 72–73

tying-down stitches 36, 37, 41, 47, 78